Getting out and staying out

Results of the prisoner Resettlement Pathfinders

Anna Clancy, Kirsty Hudson, Mike Maguire,
Richard Peake, Peter Raynor,
Maurice Vanstone and Jocelyn Kynch

First published in Great Britain in April 2006 by The Policy Press

The Policy Press
University of Bristol
Fourth Floor, Beacon House
Queen's Road
Bristol BS8 1QU
UK

Tel no +44 (0)117 331 4054
Fax no +44 (0)117 331 4093
E-mail tpp-info@bristol.ac.uk
www.policypress.org.uk

© Anna Clancy, Kirsty Hudson, Mike Maguire, Richard Peake, Peter Raynor, Maurice Vanstone and Jocelyn Kynch 2006

ISBN-10 1 86134 817 7
ISBN-13 978 1 86134 817 3

British Library Cataloguing in Publication Data
A catalogue record for this report is available from the British Library.

Library of Congress Cataloging-in-Publication Data
A catalog record for this report has been requested.

Cover design by Qube Design Associates, Bristol
Printed in Great Britain by MPG Books, Bodmin

Contents

List of tables and figures

Tables

List of figures

Acknowledgements

The authors would like to express their thanks to all members of the Pathfinder teams who put up with requests for extra data collection and gave their time to researchers for interviews and frequent discussions about their work. Equally, we thank the many offenders who agreed to be interviewed, both before and after their release, members of other agencies who provided services, and numerous Home Office staff (including those on the helpful Steering Group) who assisted with the project. In the latter context, we would like most of all to thank Steve Pitts of the National Probation Service, who was a key figure in the development and oversight of the Resettlement Pathfinders from the beginning and engaged in frequent, friendly and effective 'troubleshooting'. Finally, we are very grateful to Julie Vennard (University of Bristol), who played a leading role in the Phase 1 evaluation and undertook some interviews with senior policy makers for Phase 2, and to Andrew Rix and Steven Raybould (CRG Research), who undertook cost analyses (not published here) for the report to the Home Office.

Introduction: prisoner resettlement and the Pathfinders

The Pathfinder programme was set up by the probation service in the latter part of 1999 to pilot and evaluate new models of working with offenders. It formed an integral part of the Service's 'What Works' initiative and was originally funded under the Home Office Crime Reduction Programme.

The Resettlement Pathfinders were originally designed to test new approaches to the resettlement of adult prisoners sentenced to less than 12 months, who currently leave custody without supervision under the system of Automatic Unconditional Release (AUR). They were later extended to include young prisoners and some adults already subject to post-release supervision on licence, but the focus remained primarily on adult short-termers. This report presents an evaluation of the second (and final) phase of the Resettlement Pathfinders, based in three local prisons, in which 278 offenders voluntarily completed an innovative cognitive-motivational programme ('FOR – A Change'), obtained direct access to services to address their needs and were offered continued contact with project staff, a probation officer or a volunteer 'mentor' after release.

The report is structured as follows. The remainder of this chapter briefly introduces the problems faced by short-termers on leaving custody and shows how this group of prisoners has been neglected in comparison with others, despite its exceptionally high reconviction rates. It also outlines the main elements of the Pathfinders, summarises the findings from Phase 1 and sets out the methodology used to evaluate Phase 2. Finally, it provides a brief description of each of the three sites, the structure of the project teams and the characteristics of prisoners joining the FOR programme.

Chapter 2 examines the theoretical basis of the FOR programme and the integrity of its delivery, including assessments of quality based on observation of videos. This is complemented in Chapter 3 by an analysis of interviews with staff and prisoners about their experiences of the pre-release stage of the Pathfinders, with a focus on their views of the programme as a whole and of specific sessions within it. Chapter 4 provides an analysis of post-release issues, including the nature and extent of contact with ex-prisoners and of referrals to other agencies.

Chapter 5 presents findings relating to the impact and outcomes of the Pathfinders. This includes measures of the levels of continuity of service 'through the gate', as well as changes in crime-related attitudes and in self-assessed problems as measured by the CRIME-PICS II instrument. The latter include some post-release measures of change, which proved impossible in the first Pathfinder evaluation. A brief summary is also provided of the results of a one-year reconviction analysis of participants in Phase I of the Pathfinders, comparing actual rates of reconviction both against predicted rates (based on the OGRS2 instrument) and against comparison groups of short-term prisoners from the same prisons a year or so earlier.

Chapter 6 presents findings in relation to key implementation issues, both in the organisational arrangements and in methods of delivery of services.

Finally, Chapter 7 draws together the main findings from the study and offers some broad conclusions.

Short-term prisoners: a history of neglect

Concern about the problems faced by prisoners on their release – and the part these play in re-offending – is anything but new, yet the history of what has been called at different times 'through-care', 'aftercare' or 'resettlement' is characterised predominantly by neglect. This is particularly true of short-term prisoners, most of whom have had no access to rehabilitative interventions inside prison and little or no assistance after release. Comments from different periods illustrate a broadly unchanging pattern of problems and lack of progress in addressing them. For example, writing in the early post-war years, Leo Page (1950) commented:

> Few prisoners had adequate preparations for their release. Access to pre-release courses was patchy and many prisoners were discharged with little idea what was happening to them and with no access to support and advice.

One of the ironies in the situation is that the group which receives the least assistance has both the greatest level of social need and the highest reconviction rates. Adult prisoners serving under 12 months constitute about half of all those released from prison each year. Around 60% are reconvicted within two years and about half of these (30% overall) receive a new prison sentence. High proportions have multiple entrenched social and personal problems, most commonly relating to accommodation, finances, substance misuse, education, employment and difficulties in relationships. These problems tend to interact, creating what Corden (1983) calls a 'cycle of disadvantage'. Moreover, they are exacerbated both by imprisonment itself – which can result, for example, in the loss of existing accommodation – and by the social stigma and rejection that are often experienced by ex-prisoners. All the above issues have been documented repeatedly in research studies and inquiries over many years (see, for example, Banks and Fairhead, 1976; Corden et al, 1978, 1979; Fairhead, 1981; Home Office, 1992, 2001; NACRO, 1993, 2000; Maguire et al, 1997, 2000; Social Exclusion Unit, 2002; Lewis et al, 2003a). It has also been shown that both women (Carlen, 1983; Caddle and White, 1994; NACRO, 1996) and people from minority ethnic groups (NACRO, 2002) tend to experience even greater resettlement problems than white males.

Until the 1980s, most short-term prisoners at least had the option of requesting assistance on a voluntary basis. This had its roots in work by charitable organisations in the 19th century, notably by the Discharged Prisoners' Aid Societies (DPAS) and the Police Court and Prison Gate Missions (Bochel, 1976; Vanstone, 2004). Until the 1960s, the bulk of post-release assistance was provided by the DPAS, but from 1965 the probation service set up a formal system of 'voluntary aftercare'. In many cases this amounted to little more than advice or short-term help with pressing practical problems, but at its peak it was provided to over 10,000 prisoners a year and on occasion led to more significant and longer-term interventions. However, the growth of voluntary aftercare was sharply reversed during the 1980s and early 1990s, as the probation service experienced a major change in focus (Nellis, 1995). This involved a greater emphasis on the monitoring and control of more serious offenders and higher prioritisation of work with those under statutory orders – including medium- and long-term prisoners released under licence – whose supervision came to be governed by National Standards with clear threats of sanctions. By contrast, voluntary aftercare was officially downgraded in the probation service's list of national objectives and priorities (Home Office, 1984), hopes being expressed that the vacuum might again be filled by the voluntary sector. The numbers of prisoners offered voluntary aftercare shrank rapidly, and, in a survey conducted in the mid-1990s, Maguire et al (1997, 2000) found that the voluntary aftercare system had effectively broken down, leaving a needy and risky group almost entirely without guidance or support.

However, with the rise of government interest in the 'What Works' movement at the end of the century – which brought with it a clear focus on the issue of reducing re-offending – a new awareness of the implications of the neglect of short-term prisoners began to grow. Reports by NACRO (2000), HM Inspectors of Prisons and Probation (Home Office, 2001), John Halliday (2001) and the Social Exclusion Unit (2002) all drew attention to their exceptionally high reconviction rates and the urgent need for interventions to improve their chances of rehabilitation. This burst of official attention not only raised the profile of programmes such as the Resettlement Pathfinders, but culminated in legislation to ensure that, for the first time, the majority of people who spend a short time in prison will become subject to statutory supervision after release. The new 'Custody Plus' sentence, to be introduced from 2007 under the 2003 Criminal Justice Act, will consist of a short period in custody followed by a lengthy period of supervision in the community, the aim being to produce a 'seamless' transition between the two stages of the sentence. Offenders subject to Custody Plus will also be subject to the new 'end-to-end' offender management system outlined in the National Offender Management Model, which should in theory result in more effective supervision based on strong continuity of relationships between offenders and their 'managers' (although for a sceptical view, see Raynor and Maguire, 2006). While differing from Custody Plus in the important respect that participation was voluntary, the Pathfinder projects were similar enough in purpose (not least, in placing high priority on the aim of reducing re-offending) to throw some light on issues of principle and practice that are likely to emerge when the new sentence is introduced.

The Resettlement Pathfinders and the 'FOR – A Change' programme

The Pathfinders were implemented and evaluated in two separate phases. Phase I initially involved six projects run in partnership with the prison service, each based in a local prison. Three were managed by voluntary organisations, the other three (one of them based in a women's prison) being probation-led. A seventh project – also probation-led, but based in a private prison – was added in early 2001.

During the course of Phase I, an extra element was incorporated into three of the four probation-led projects, namely the 'FOR – A Change' programme. Also known simply as FOR (which stands for 'Focus on Resettlement'), this is a short cognitive-motivational programme intended to equip prisoners with better thinking skills and greater motivation to make use of services, and hence to improve their prospects of successful resettlement and desistance from crime. The choice of this programme was influenced by a desire on the part of Pathfinder policy makers to move beyond simply providing 'welfare' services to ex-prisoners, towards the more ambitious aim of significantly reducing their rates of re-offending – an aim compatible with that of the broader 'What Works' initiative (the Crime Reduction Programme) within which the Pathfinders were devised. The designers of FOR drew on established cognitive-behavioural (CB) principles, which underpinned many of the other prison and probation programmes funded under the Crime Reduction Programme (CRP), and about which there was a substantial body of evidence to suggest that they could be effective in this regard (see, for example, Ross and Fabiano, 1985; McGuire, 1995; Goldblatt and Lewis, 1998). However, it was recognised that short-termers did not spend sufficient time in custody to allow them to complete the requisite number of hours – or 'dosage' – usually recognised by psychologists as necessary if a CB programme is to have a fundamental impact on thinking (this is also a criterion for official accreditation: see CSAP, 2004). Hence, rather than try to produce an intensive 'mini' CB programme, it was felt that it would be of more value to design a new programme incorporating CB principles, but with a particular focus on motivation and on practical problem solving. The FOR programme consisted initially of 12 sessions designed for delivery in the prison plus a more individualised component for follow-up use in the community (an optional session

13 has since been added). During Phase 1, a total of 1,081 prisoners participated in the Pathfinders, of whom 114 completed the FOR programme.

Phase 1 results

An evaluation of Phase 1 was published in 2003 by Lewis et al (2003a, 2003b). This included analysis of the resettlement problems faced by the participants, and of the kinds and levels of service they received. It also drew attention to key organisational and implementation issues, including assessment, case management and integration of services between partner agencies – all areas in which there was considerable variation between the projects. At that point, it was too early to determine the reconviction rates of participants, and the outcomes of the projects were measured in terms of levels of continuity (that is, the extent to which prisoners who used Pathfinder services in the prison remained in contact with the projects after release), changes in attitudes and beliefs supportive of offending and changes in self-reported life problems (both as measured by before-and-after administration of CRIME-PICS II: see Frude et al, 1994). The pattern of results for all three measures was broadly similar. All the projects achieved better continuity than the old system of 'voluntary aftercare' (as measured by Maguire et al, 1997), but there were wide variations between them: significantly higher levels of continuity were achieved by the probation-led projects, and with prisoners who had undertaken the FOR programme. Positive changes in attitudes and beliefs about crime were also associated with probation-run projects, with high service inputs and with participation in the programme; changes in self-reported problems showed broadly similar trends but fewer statistically significant differences.

Phase 2: the current study

Phase 2 of the Pathfinders, which is the subject of the evaluation presented here, was implemented in only three of the original seven prisons (Hull, Lewes and Parc), all of them holding only male prisoners. We are therefore unable to say much here about the resettlement of female offenders, although this was discussed in the Phase 1 evaluation report (Lewis et al, 2003a). The project managers of the Hull, Lewes and Parc Pathfinders were given new resources to develop and refine their work, and were encouraged to focus more strongly on the goal of reducing re-offending and on interventions and practices thought likely to achieve this. In Lewes, particularly, this entailed more ambitious modes of working, directed at offenders' mental processes and attitudes, and moving well beyond simply the provision of 'welfare' services. In all three projects, attendance at the FOR programme (itself slightly revised since the original version) was made a condition of participation, staff were trained in motivational interviewing and attempts were made to provide more consistent assessment and case management. In addition to short-termers, there was some delivery of the programme to prisoners serving over 12 months (but less than four years) and to young offenders; both of these groups are subject to statutory supervision. In total, 278 prisoners completed the programme and were released from prison within the evaluation period, which ended in July 2003.

This study provides both a descriptive account of the work of these second-stage Pathfinders, and an evaluation of their performance using the same key outcome measures as in the first study, namely continuity, attitude change and problem change. There is a stronger focus on the FOR programme and the experiences of those delivering it and experiencing it. In addition, greater attention is paid to post-release experiences, which were much better documented by the projects in Phase 2; the team also conducted 71 interviews with offenders after their release.

The evaluation used a variety of data sources and methods of analysis, which are described in more detail at appropriate points in the text. The most important sources of data were:

- routine completion by members of the three Pathfinders of a case management record (CMR) for each prisoner joining the FOR programme, using a form specially designed for the purpose by the research team. This included post-release as well as pre-release activities;
- an OASys (Offender Assessment System) assessment completed by the projects for each participant (OASys is the standard tool used in England and Wales to assess offenders' needs and level of risk);
- administrations of an attitudes questionnaire, CRIME-PICS II, in prison, before and after prisoners attended the programme, and subsequently a third administration, where possible, after release;
- interviews with all members of the Pathfinder teams in the three sites, including the 'community links' responsible for the post-release stage of the resettlement process;
- telephone interviews with representatives of 24 agencies providing post-release services to offenders;
- pre-release interviews with 163 prisoners who participated in the FOR programme;
- interviews with 71 of the above prisoners after their release;
- observation and rating of video recordings of 47 group and individual sessions of the FOR programme;
- interviews with six senior policy managers from the prison and probation services.

The above data were analysed mainly in order to:

(a) provide a picture of the ways in which the resettlement process, including the FOR programme, was organised and delivered in each of the three prisons and after prisoners' release;

(b) gather and examine the views and experiences of a variety of 'key players' in the process, including project staff, prisoners and members of outside service agencies;

(c) produce interim (proxy) indicators of the outcomes of the resettlement process in Phase 2, in advance of a possible later reconviction study.

Finally, details of all offenders who took part in the Phase 1 Pathfinders were run through the Home Office Offenders Index to determine one-year reconviction rates for the original seven pilot projects. These were compared with the reconviction rates of randomly selected groups of short-term prisoners who had been released from the same establishments a year or so earlier. The results of this analysis are presented briefly in Chapter 5.

Second, much of the basic data for the study was collected by project staff rather than the researchers: in particular, we relied heavily on CMRs designed by ourselves but filled in by managers, facilitators and community links. These records were completed more fully in Phase 2 than they had been in Phase 1, but a certain amount of data was missing, particularly in relation to activities after release. In addition, OASys and CRIME-PICS II assessments were not completed on every participant (although, again, there was a major improvement in comparison to Phase 1). Altogether, 301 of the 352 prisoners who started FOR – 266 of the 278 who eventually completed it, and 35 of the 74 who dropped out – had an OASys assessment. These missing data may distort some of the findings, especially concerning the characteristics of 'starters' as a whole. However, in general we are confident that most failures to assess people or fill in records were caused simply by pressures of time, and that there was no systematic bias in data recording at an individual level. The only major bias caused by missing data is likely to concern our own interviews with ex-prisoners, and third administrations of CRIME-PICS after release. As noted above, we interviewed a (reasonably representative) sample of 163 participants in prison, but managed to locate and re-interview only 71 of them after release. It is probable that the latter 71 were as a group both more settled in the community and more likely to have desisted from crime than the 92 we failed to re-interview.

The Pathfinder sites, project teams and prisoners

This section provides an introductory overview of the three sites at which the FOR programme was delivered, the types of staff involved in the projects (including links for post-release work) and the characteristics and assessed needs of the offenders who participated. More detailed discussion of organisational issues around staffing, prisoner recruitment and programme and service delivery will be found in later chapters.

HMP Parc

HMP Parc is a private Category B local prison housing approximately 900 male adult and young offenders. The prison has a reputation for running a progressive regime, which offers prisoners a wide range of activities and courses. The Offending Behaviour Programmes Unit is responsible for delivering all programmes within the prison. At the time of the study, the unit was managed by a senior probation officer, and the staff comprised both probation and prison officers. Seven were trained as FOR tutors, including one prison officer responsible for managing the programme. The unit had been running the FOR programme continuously since it joined Phase 1 of the Resettlement Pathfinders in 2001.

To be eligible for the programme, prisoners had to be:

- resettling within the South Wales probation area;
- serving a sentence of less than four years;
- nearing their release date.

In Phase 1, which involved relatively few prisoners, FOR staff from the prison undertook much of the post-release work themselves in an ad hoc fashion, but in Phase 2 the programme was linked up with FOR-trained probation officers based at five probation offices across South Wales. At the start of each programme these officers were provided with the names and release dates of prisoners returning to their area and asked to attend session 12, the Marketplace session, along with a number of service providers. The initial plan was for all ACR prisoners joining the programme (that is, those subject to Automatic Conditional Release with statutory supervision) to be allocated to one of the FOR-trained probation officers for supervision on licence, but practical problems meant that this did not always happen.

HMP Hull

HMP Hull is a Category B local prison, remand centre and young offender institution, serving Hull and surrounding East Yorkshire. It has recently undergone major structural changes and a new wing was opened in November 2002, adding an extra 350 places. This gives an operational capacity of just over 1,000 places, approximately 115 of which are for young offenders.

The Pathfinder team contained a mix of probation and prison staff, including a senior prison officer, a probation officer (the treatment manager) and a number of probation support officers and prison officers. However, most of these were recruited on short-term secondments and the staffing situation was uncertain and in flux for long periods, which caused considerable problems and frustrations for the project team (see Chapter 6).

To be eligible for the programme all prisoners had to be:

- serving less than four years and within the last three months of their sentence (or due for Home Detention Curfew within three months);
- resettling in the local catchment area.

Post-release contact in the community was conducted by the FOR staff rather than by a community probation officer. One of the programme facilitators was responsible for holding a weekly surgery every Friday at the local probation office. All post-release progress was subsequently recorded on the CMRs by FOR staff on their return to the prison.

HMP Lewes

As a local prison, HMP Lewes houses mainly short-term prisoners and remands. Since March 2002 it has ceased to receive and hold young offenders, but a small group of such prisoners are held at a remand facility on the same site, which serves the local courts in the East and West Sussex area. The capacity of the prison is 546 inmates.

The FOR programme was available to participants in HMP Lewes between July 2002 and July 2003. It was run by the Crime Reduction Initiative (CRI), a voluntary organisation that has experience of working with offenders in custody and in the community.

To be eligible for the programme, prisoners were required to be:

- serving a sentence of less than four years;
- nearing their release date;
- resettling in Brighton, Eastbourne or Worthing.

Owing to shortfalls against target numbers, in certain circumstances these conditions were waived: for example, offenders who did not wish to settle in one of the three catchment areas were sometimes accepted if willing to travel to maintain post-release contact.

The resettlement manager, who also oversaw the delivery of the FOR programme, was responsible for bridging the gap between the prison and the community, and for post-release contact with participants in the Brighton area. (In Phase 1, Lewes had used mentors for post-release work, but these had left during the hiatus between Phase 1 and Phase 2.) He was later assisted by a community link officer seconded to the programme on a part-time basis from Sussex probation service. Prisoners who planned to return to either Worthing or Eastbourne were supervised by two community workers in each area.

Prisoner profiles: characteristics and needs

This section provides basic profiles of the prisoners who participated in the FOR programme in each of the three sites. Details presented include their age, ethnicity, and 'problems and needs', as identified via OASys and CRIME-PICS II assessments.

Numbers of participants

According to the projects' CMRs, a total of 352 prisoners attended at least one session of the FOR programme during Phase 2 of the Pathfinders, and 278 (79%) of these went on to complete the programme. Table 1.1 shows the throughput of prisoners in each of the three sites. It can be seen that Parc was more successful than the other two prisons in terms of completions, and that, in all three sites, ACR prisoners were marginally more likely to complete than AUR prisoners. The only category with a poor completion rate was that of young offenders in Hull, where only nine out of 17 completed. Factors contributing to attrition are discussed in Chapter 6.

In the light of the complex targeting arrangements, and an absence of relevant information from the prisons, it is not possible to calculate what proportion of all those prisoners eligible to join the programme actually took advantage of the opportunity. However, in Phase 1 it was estimated that, in two of the prisons delivering the programme, about 10% of all those eligible took part and completed it. The equivalent figure is likely to have been considerably higher than this (perhaps double) in Phase 2, at least for short-term prisoners.

Age and ethnic group

The age profiles of prisoners in Hull and Parc were relatively similar, with approximately 50% of participants aged under 25 and around one in 10 aged over 35. Participants in Lewes tended to be older, with 28% aged under 25 and 30% aged over 35.

More importantly, participants across all three sites were almost exclusively white, indicating that members of black and minority ethnic groups were under-represented in all three programmes in relation to the prison population. This problem – which has also been noted in relation to prison programmes more generally (NACRO, 2002; Powis and Walmsley, 2002; Calverley et al, 2004) – clearly raises questions about equity and possible discrimination. It is also important because black and minority ethnic prisoners have consistently been found to have more acute resettlement problems than white prisoners (see, for example, Maguire et al, 1997, 2000; NACRO, 2000, 2002; Calverley et al, 2004).

Table 1.1: Throughput of prisoners on FOR programme: February 2002–July 2003[a,b]

HMP Parc			
Sentence type	Number starting	Number completing	Number non-completers	% completing
AUR[c]	57	51	6	89
ACR[d]	52	49	3	94
YO[e]	24	20	4	83
Total	133	120	13	90
HMP Hull				
Sentence type	Number starting	Number completing	Number non-completers	% completing
AUR	78	57	21	73
ACR	31	25	6	81
YO	17	9	8	47
Total	126	91	35	72
HMP Lewes				
Sentence type	Number starting	Number completing	Number non-completers	% completing
AUR	63	45	18	71
ACR	30	22	8	73
YO	0	0	0	n/a
Total	93	67	26	72
All				
Sentence type	Number starting	Number completing	Number non-completers	% completing
AUR	198	153	45	77
ACR	113	96	17	85
YO	41	29	12	71
Total	352	278	74	79

Notes:

[a] Parc is the only site to have run the FOR programme on a continuous basis since the first Pathfinders. Hull began running it again from July 2002, while Lewes ran it for the first time in that month.

[b] A prisoner is counted as having started if he attends session 1.

[c] AUR = serving less than 12 months and not subject to statutory licence.

[d] ACR = serving 12 months or over and less than 4 years, and subject to statutory licence.

[e] YO = young offenders.

Problems and needs

Prisoners were assessed using two instruments to measure their problems and needs, namely the OASys and CRIME-PICS II tools. OASys is the standard offender assessment system developed by the Home Office, which is now being used to assess risks and needs in all prisons and probation areas. CRIME-PICS II (Frude et al, 1994) is an instrument that measures attitudes to crime (G score) and the level of practical and emotional problems offenders face (P score).

Overall, participants scored high on both instruments relative to offender groups measured in other studies, reflecting the general finding that short-term prisoners tend to have major social needs. Participants in Parc prison had lower mean scores than those in the other prisons on all three scales analysed, indicating lower levels of problems, and attitudes less favourable to crime. By contrast, Hull prisoners had particularly high scores on OASys, while Lewes scored highest on the CRIME-PICS II 'Problems' scale (see Appendix A, Tables A1 to A3). The extent of change in scores among those who were reassessed after completing the FOR programme – used as a proxy for reconviction rates – is discussed in Chapter 5.

Table 1.2 shows the percentages of Pathfinder participants in each prison who were assessed through OASys as having 'significant' problems of specific kinds (that is, scoring higher than the 'cut-off point', above which the authors calculate that there is a dynamic risk factor present that may impact on re-offending – see NPS, 2001, p 116). The problems appearing most frequently were 'lifestyle and associates' and 'drug misuse', both of which were attributed to over half of those assessed in all three sites. However, there was considerable variation in other problems between the prisons. For example, 'accommodation' was identified as the most common problem of all among Lewes prisoners (assessed as significant in 64% of cases), but considerably less frequent in both Hull (45%) and Parc (37%). This is consistent with findings in the Phase 1 evaluation, and probably reflects differences in housing markets between the south east of England and the South Yorkshire and South Wales areas. More difficult to explain are the differences between Hull and Lewes, especially in OASys scores of problems relating to 'Attitudes' (assessed as significant for 73% of prisoners in Hull, 28% in Lewes) and 'Thinking and behaviour' (59% in Hull, 17% in Lewes). Similar inconsistencies were reported in the Phase 1 Pathfinders study in relation to both Lewes and another voluntary-led project (Lewis et al, 2003a, p 33). The most likely explanation seems to be that staff from voluntary agencies with expertise in practical 'welfare' issues are by training and culture more likely to focus their attention upon prisoners' practical needs, while staff in the probation-led programmes (again because of their training, occupational culture and experience) tend to be more aware of cognitive deficits: in other words, such differences may be reflected in the way they score OASys. This may be a finding that deserves wider attention, given the status of OASys as the standard offender assessment instrument.

Table 1.2: OASys results: participants with 'significant' problems (%)[a]

Type of problem	Parc	Lewes	Hull	All sites
Lifestyle and associates	75	63	86	75[b]
Drug misuse	53	62	69	69
Attitudes	50	28	73	52[b]
Accommodation	37	64	45	47[b]
Education, training and employability	35	42	57	44[b]
Thinking and behaviour	39	17	59	40[b]
Financial management and income	38	28	29	32
Relationships	34	40	25	32
Emotional well-being	32	26	22	27
Alcohol misuse	28	27	18	24

Notes:
$n = 301$.
[a] In OASys, each problem is scored individually and a threshold score is set at which the offender is considered to have a 'significant' problem in that area.
[b] Chi-square test shows a significant statistical relationship between prison and proportion of participants with a 'significant' problem of the type shown ($p < .05$).

Finally, in addition to OASys assessments, the research team gleaned information about two of the main problems faced by short-term prisoners – unemployment and lack of suitable accommodation – from entries in their CMRs. Only 15% of participants in Hull stated that they had been employed at the time of their arrest, compared with 29% in Parc and 27% in Lewes. Fewer than half of participants across all three sites had been living in permanent accommodation. Data on prisoners' expected post-release employment and accommodation status at the time of their first assessment in prison, show that even fewer expected to obtain jobs or permanent accommodation following their release (see Appendix A, Tables A4 and A5).

2

The 'FOR – A Change' programme and its delivery

I n this chapter and the next, we look more closely at the FOR programme and at the way in which it was delivered by the project staff and received by offenders. Particular attention is paid to the theoretical foundations of the programme and to the integrity with which the designers' intentions were realised in practice. This chapter focuses on findings from observational research; Chapter 3 examines the programme (as well as other aspects of the project) through the eyes of staff and prisoners.

Theoretical foundations of the programme

'FOR – A Change' (Fabiano and Porporino, 2002) is a 13-session programme[1] based on the concept of motivational interviewing developed by Miller and Rollnick (1991). It derives from the programme authors' conclusion that to date, while the 'What Works' movement has focused appropriately on, for instance, problem solving and thinking skills, it has not as yet concerned itself sufficiently with motivation.[2] In their view, this leaves attempts to change offenders vulnerable to erosion, either because ambivalence about change has not been addressed or because newly acquired skills have not been reinforced. In this respect they echo the findings of other effectiveness research, which concludes that initial effect can be undermined by a lack of post-programme reinforcement (Raynor and Vanstone, 1996). The programme draws on the principle that 'key "transitions" can interrupt life "trajectories" that have been consistently criminal and anti-social in character' (Fabiano and Porporino, 2002, p 1) and that therefore interventions should motivate offenders towards goals that produce transitions. Its primary objective is to increase motivation so that programme participants establish their own agenda for change. If successful, it is proposed, they will be more likely to seek appropriate help after the programme, more willing to focus on offending and more likely to

---

[1] A list of the headings of the 13 sessions is given in Appendix B.

[2] A similar conclusion, it is worth noting, has been reached via a very different route by proponents of 'desistance' theory, such as Maruna (2000) and Farrall (2002), who tend to be hostile to cognitive-behavioural programmes, but emphasise the importance of motivation to change processes. For a recent discussion of the relevance of desistance theory to resettlement practice, see Maguire and Raynor (2006).

develop a stable lifestyle. Motivation is, therefore, implicitly a dynamic factor open to influence.

The approach is client-centred inasmuch as it is focused on the offender's agenda, but it is also directive to the extent that it 'is intentionally addressed to the resolution of ambivalence, often in a particular direction of change' (Miller and Rollnick, 2002, p 25). Thus, although it is not confrontational, it is challenging within the subtle definition provided by Egan (1990), and it is reliant on the directive style of group leadership advocated in the 'What Works' literature (Ross et al, 1986), namely one that avoids being didactic but encourages discussion and exchange of ideas. Miller and Rollnick (2002) emphasise that while it is client-centred it is also directive because it is concerned with helping the individual towards change; however, this is not authoritarian but rather the subtler tipping of a balance. Moreover, it is 'a method of communication rather than a set of techniques' (p 25). This method involves collaboration (exploration and support in a partnership); evocation (eliciting and drawing out the individual's own resources and motivation); and autonomy (affirmation of the individual's 'right and capacity for self-direction'). This fits very much with Ginsburg et al's (2002) view that a coercive model makes the development of rapport between worker and offender difficult.

Throughout the programme, the group members are encouraged to think of their life as a journey (trajectory), and then guided through five stages, namely:

- acceptance of the need for change;
- problem recognition;
- problem definition;
- setting a plan for change;
- controlling for risks of relapse.

Briefly, the programme is structured around the programme participant's current state, desired future state and the setting of goals and a plan for change. The process involves work on factors relating to perception; interpretation; attitudes; values that might inhibit or enhance change; the setting of goals relevant to offending histories; relapse prevention; and access to community resources.

The ethos within which this process occurs is crucial because, as Miller and Rollnick (2002, p 12) assert, '[i]ntrinsic motivation for change arises in an accepting, empowering atmosphere that makes it safe for the person to explore the possibly painful present in relation to what is wanted and valued'. The creation of such an ethos is helped by the application of four guiding principles:

- expressing empathy through skilful, reflective listening;
- developing discrepancy between the current state and desired state;
- rolling with, rather than opposing, resistance;
- supporting self-efficacy or belief in the capacity for change.

Essentially, then, it is based on a partnership between facilitator and participant.

Programme integrity

The term 'programme integrity' refers to the extent to which those delivering a programme do so in tune with, as it were, both the letter and the spirit intended by its designers. Our approach to checking programme integrity was based on three main sources of data:

- observation of a selection of videos using a number of integrity checklists;
- interviews with offenders (to produce some structured participant feedback on aspects of programme delivery);
- interviews with managers (which included a focus on the implementation of the programme).

This chapter first outlines the rationale for our approach and its associated methodology, as well as its limitations, then presents the findings of the observational analysis. The results of interviews with staff and offenders are presented in Chapter 3.

Rationale, scope and limitations

Our general approach was informed partly by the experience of evaluating the delivery of the FOR programme in Parc Prison during the first phase of the resettlement evaluation, partly by previous experience of checking programme integrity in the Straight Thinking on Probation (STOP) experiment (Raynor and Vanstone, 1996), and partly by relevant literature on programme integrity (Ross and Fabiano, 1985; Hollin, 1995, 2001; McGuire, 1995; Bernfeld, 2001; Bonta et al, 2001; Gendreau et al, 2001).

The literature clearly tells us that programme integrity is broader than the simple mechanism of delivering the programme. The definition of programme integrity relied on here is that of Ross and Fabiano (1985) in their original exposition of the cognitive-behavioural model:

> [the programme] is of sufficient duration and sufficient intensity and [...] conforms to the program principles [and the trainers] actually provide the program they are supposed to provide. (p 199)

They argue that the performance of the programme leaders is linked inextricably to the motivation of programme participants:

> Interpersonal skills of the trainers and the way they are trained to teach these techniques will determine whether they are successful in overcoming [...] poor motivation. (p 197)

They also state that it is 'axiomatic' that the effectiveness of programmes is dependent 'in large measure' on the skill level of the trainer (p 198). Other commentators have broadened our understanding of how these principles operate in practice. First, Hollin (1995) outlines three basic threats to programme integrity: programme drift (an incremental change in the aim of a programme); programme reversal (the undermining of the programme approach – for instance, demotivating rather than motivating); and programme non-compliance (changes to, or omissions from, the programme). Second, Bernfeld (2001) stresses that challenges to the proper implementation of programmes occur potentially at four levels: client level (inaccurate matching of treatment and trainers to client); programme level (the lack of a shared 'superordinate' goal within the particular agency); organisational level (for example, the lack of a coherent management philosophy); and societal level (for example, counterproductive government policy). Finally, Gendreau et al (2001) argue the need in the implementation of programmes for attention to four elements:

* organisational factors (for example, experience of innovation);
* programme factors (for example, cost-effectiveness);
* consultancy;
* staff characteristics (for example, belief in the programme).

These features of the literature provide a context for the clarification of what we believe can and cannot be achieved in this aspect of the evaluation. It is beyond the scope of the evaluation to assess the qualities of individual group leaders other than from implications drawn from certain outcomes, such as levels of interaction within the group, atmosphere of the session, and so on. Moreover, because the cameras were focused on the group leaders, it was possible only to judge the verbal contributions of the programme participants, and it was not possible to judge the level of motivation of each group member (except to assume that it is probable that individual participants were at different stages of the motivational cycle). Nevertheless, it was possible to draw some conclusions about the quality of group response. Finally, while it is possible that the study as a whole can throw some light on each of the levels referred to by Bernfeld, and the factors described by Gendreau et al, the analysis of practice is most appropriately focused on Hollin's three threats to programme integrity.

Accordingly, recordings of work (within the three prisons), which represent the application of the general sessions and of pivotal points in the programme (namely, sessions 7 and 13), were observed in a systematic fashion. In all, 47 recordings of sessions were viewed (18 from Hull, 14 from Lewes and 15 from Parc), drawn from 17 groups run between September 2002 and July 2003 by 16 programme facilitators. Observation was aided by the use of two checklists – one for the group sessions, and one for session 7. In addition, 17 workbooks were read. Random sampling was not possible, so we cannot be certain that the recordings viewed are representative; however, the tapes were secured through a variety of sources (the prisons, the Home Office and the programme designers, T3 Associates) and they provide at least one example of each session of the programme. In addition, five post-release sessions were either observed or listened to and a sample of workbooks was read. Discussion took place between the observer and the treatment manager from T3, and comparisons were possible between five core leaders observed by both.

Programme drift

As indicated above, the broad focus of the programme is on motivating offenders towards goals that change their life trajectories in ways that divert them away from criminal and anti-social behaviour (criminogenic goals). This broad focus can only be maintained if the focus of each individual session is adhered to. Of the 47 sessions observed, 43 were adjudged to have kept, and the other four to have partly kept, the required focus. Two of the latter occurred early on in the sequence of groups, and the missing of some important aspects of the session probably reflects the inexperience of the group leaders. The other two were final sessions in which the demands of the institution shortened the session, with the result that some exercises were omitted. However, our overall assessment, based on observations of sessions covering a period of nearly 12 months, is that 16 facilitators in three different environments managed to avoid any corrosive changes in the programme. This is attributable partly to their adherence to the requirements of the manual, but it is also attributable to a strong programme design and very clear structure within which to work.

A further indication of the maintenance of the broad programme aim is the nature of the goals stimulated by the programme. As Table 2.1 shows, 17 workbooks by participants from five groups in the three prisons, chosen at random (although not necessarily representative), illustrate a familiar range of goals related to criminogenic needs.

Table 2.1: Needs addressed by goals defined in 17 workbooks

Employment/training	16
Accommodation/housing	13
Alcohol/drugs	12
Family/relationships	11
Staying out of trouble/prison	7
Changing lifestyle	6
Increasing confidence/self-respect	6
Health/fitness	5
Money	4
Keeping focused on change	3
Driving legally	2
Gambling	2
Controlling temper	1

The following extract from a workbook illustrates how goals are linked to action steps:

Goal	Good job
Action steps	Look in job centre, look in papers, ask family and friends
Goal	Manage drugs
Action steps	Drug counsellor, detox, agency support, talk to family and friends, stay away from bad friends
Goal	Stop gambling
Action steps	Agency support, stay out of arcades, family support
Goal	Keep focused
Action steps	Leave girls who got boyfriends, focus my brain
Goal	Stop driving illegally
Action steps	Think of people, don't buy any cars, think of prison

The process of setting such goals is based on personal reflection about the offender's current 'story' and the desired future story. The following extract from the workbook of a man convicted of possession of Class A drugs provides a vivid contrast between a crime-related life and a crime-free life.

My story
My father died when I was two years old. My mother and gran have brought me and my brother up. They have never seen us as wrong. They have always been there for me. I started smoking drugs when I was about 12-13 and then moved on to other drugs, and then started to sell and abuse them. When I was 17 I accidentally burnt my house down and nearly died. I was sleeping in the house with the chip pan on. I was sleeping for about an hour and then the fire engine people woke me up. Then when I was 18 I had my first daughter [...]. Then had my second daughter at the age of 23. Her name is [...].

My story: the future
To have a son and see my children grow up and maybe have some grandchildren and maybe have a business of my own and a bit of money to help them out in life.

Programme reversal

In one of the first groups run in Lewes (where FOR was introduced for the first time in 2002), the trainers seemed to be hesitant and unfamiliar with the material, lacking in confidence, passive and almost mechanistic in approach and, more importantly, lacking belief in the programme. However, observation over the full period of the evaluation showed that these trainers – boosted by experience and in-house training – greatly increased their confidence and knowledge of the programme. As discussed in Chapter 3, the staff themselves confirmed this in interviews, while the overall sense from the observations that the tutors in all three sites believed in the programme is given further credence by the fact that those interviewed all found it forward-looking and stimulating.

Leaders are required to follow the basic principles of motivational interviewing:

- express empathy;
- develop any discrepancy;
- avoid argument/roll with resistance;
- support self-efficacy

and also to avoid a number of traps:

- ordering;
- warning;

- advising;
- lecturing;
- preaching;
- judging;
- ridiculing or shaming;
- reassuring;
- distracting or changing the subject;
- interpreting or analysing;
- questioning and probing.

In every observed session, the facilitators adhered broadly to these principles and avoided the traps. Of course, the degree to which facilitators were reflective and used effective listening techniques varied, but, as comparison with the observations on five of the facilitators by the programme quality manager confirms, facilitators were functioning within a broad motivational style. Each facilitator appeared to be familiar with the material (sometimes aided by notes) and guided by the basic principles of motivational interviewing, avoiding, for instance, argument, giving advice, moralising and being judgemental. Moreover, they dealt appropriately with any verbal resistance (non-verbal resistance was beyond the scope of the observation), encouraged a positive approach to the process of change and maintained a focus on criminogenic need.

There were some good examples of adherence to the four general principles of motivational work – expressing empathy; developing discrepancy; rolling with resistance; and supporting self-efficacy.

Expressing empathy

- A facilitator, after implying that she works at the pace of the group and with their estimation of change, asks, 'Does it [the resolution of a particular problem] matter to you?' and, in response to an affirmative reply, 'then it is important'.
- In a session 1:
  Participant: 'It's not easy to get off drugs.'
  Facilitator: 'Not easy, but you can change your life.'
- In a session 7, the facilitator listens to the participant retell parts of his story and restate goals, then says, 'You know yourself better than anyone. What would stop you achieving your goals?'

Develop any discrepancy

- In a session 7, a participant who is in prison for (among other things) driving while disqualified and still owns a car, stresses the goal of getting married. The facilitator helps him explore the relationship between further illegal driving (the present behaviour – thinking about getting in the car when he is released) and the achievement or otherwise of his goal of getting married (future desired state).
- In another session 7:
  Facilitator: 'What brought you in this time? What happened?'
  Participant describes using drugs and alcohol and this leading to him committing a burglary, and then says: 'I'm not a burglar, it's despicable.'
  Facilitator: 'But despite you thinking it's despicable, you did it.'
  Participant: 'Yeah, out of my head.'
  Facilitator: 'So, what will keep you out of trouble is not using?'
- Again in a session 7, a participant who has stated making sure the family enjoy Christmas describes his violence as 'triggered' and beyond his control:
  Facilitator: 'How concerned are you about this on a scale of 1 to 10?'
  Participant: 'It's something I've got to live with.'
  Facilitator: 'How has that affected or influenced family support?'

Avoid argument/roll with resistance

- A participant insists that he would rather draw benefits than work and the facilitator avoids getting drawn into challenging that position.
- In discussion of a scenario from a session 5, no one in the group will consider 'grassing'. The facilitator resists being drawn in and moves on to discussion about standing by values.
- In a session 8, when discussing a fictional case (James) the group develops an argument about the respective dangers of alcohol and other drugs. The facilitator allows a short discussion, and then intervenes:
  'Right, let's get back to poor James then.'
- *Facilitator:* 'What's important to you?'
  Participant: 'Anything.' (Keeps repeating the response.)
  Facilitator: (To the group as a whole) 'Can you always tell when something's important to you?'
  Participant: Makes several flippant, humorous comments.
  Facilitator: (Smiling) 'You know, he's been like this for the last three days. There's no dealing with him.' (Moves on.)

Support self-efficacy

- A facilitator used an illustration of a former participant who came back to prison, but nevertheless had stayed drug-free when out.
- Facilitators used positive affirmation frequently as a way of encouraging participation, but it also contributes to increasing confidence in the skills required for change, as in the following example:

  Participant: 'What I want to know is how you can turn it around to think differently?'

  Facilitator: 'Thank you K. We are going to look at how we get over roadblocks. Thanks for that. You can't put it clearer and better than K has just said. Good point! Good point!'
- Participant: 'I've never felt so strong on anything. I've got a little baby now and I feel it, I feel it in my head. I just know that my baby is more important to me than drink. I just know that.'

  Facilitator: 'That in itself is as strong and as good a reason to achieve that goal you've set yourself as anything I've ever heard.'
- At the end of a session 1:

  Facilitator: 'The first session – you've done an awful lot. You ought to be really proud of yourselves. You've really worked very hard. We did say that parts were very difficult, but you've proved that you can do it.'

Reinforcement of learning is built into the structure of the programme, and this is another of its strengths. Thus, facilitators are encouraged to refer back to previous learning. This was noted in observation, and facilitators were judged to have referred often to previous learning if they did so as required by the manual, very often if they did so more than required and seldom if less than required. In the 25 sessions where this was appropriate,[3] previous learning was referred to very often in six sessions, often in 15 sessions and seldom in four sessions. Significantly, those sessions in which referral back to previous learning was low were early sessions in which the facilitators' confidence and familiarity with the material was low; observation of the same facilitators in later programmes revealed appropriate levels of referral back to previous learning.

Inevitably, the trainers differed in approach, some being more methodical and detailed; and each helped the participants to consider change and produce goals that broadly correlated with the definition SMART (specific, meaningful, achievable/accessible, realistic, timely) and were directed at reducing offending. At their most impressive, facilitators were very familiar and at ease with the course material and, while adhering meticulously to the content of the manual, 'worked' the material in a way that conveyed confidence, belief and an understanding of the principles

---

[3] Sessions 1 and 7 are excluded – session 7 because previous learning is implicit in the focus on stated goals.

of motivation building. Moreover, they positively affirmed the contributions of the participants, placing emphasis on their hard work and openness, and paid appropriate attention to the maintenance of group cohesion and dynamic. At their least impressive, the facilitators were conscientious, methodical and committed to taking the group through the basic structure of the session. The leaders could be placed on a continuum from highly proficient to competent; some were lively and animated and some were more passive. The point is that the groups responded to each of these different approaches, and this is further confirmation of the robustness of the design of the programme. In addition, it might be evidence of the fact that, although none of the group leaders were forcefully directive, they were all directive in the sense urged by Miller and Rollnick (2002) and guided participants towards an agenda of change.

Interestingly, however, it was in the 'most impressive' category that the leadership was most reminiscent of the directive style required in the Reasoning and Rehabilitation programme, and appeared most in danger of drifting away from the kind of directiveness urged by Miller and Rollnick towards a more didactic, less reflective, style. Indeed, the T3 treatment manager picked up the same point in feedback to a confident facilitator who at times appeared to be 'telling' participants what to do. There is, then, occasionally a sense in which there might be 'too much' coming from the leader that borders on persuasion; but clearly there is a thin line between conveying belief and persuading, and the generally high level of engagement of participants in the process suggests that the trainers achieved the right kind of balance.

Indeed, the general adherence to the appropriate style opened up the challenging nature of the programme itself. This is illustrated graphically by the following example. After an hour of the first session of one group led by a competent, methodical facilitator and in which the group participants had been encouraged to answer the question 'Who are you?' and begin to think about their life story, a participant said without criticism:

> 'It tests us. This is the first time I've felt as challenged as this in ages. This first hour has been cruel, you know what I mean.'

This reflects the implicit aim of subtly encouraging self-challenge and reflection, as opposed to engaging in confrontation, which the facilitators are trained to avoid.

Further direct evidence of the degree to which facilitators sustained the broad aim of the programme (and thereby avoided programme reversal) is discernible in the level of interaction in, and contribution from, the participants and the pervading atmosphere of the groups. Inevitably, there is a degree of subjectivity in such judgements but the observer was guided by how consistently the participants responded to prompts from the facilitators, involved themselves in the exercises and how engaged in the focus of the sessions they were. In 25 group sessions and one Marketplace, on a rating from 1 (very low) to 4 (very high), 24 were rated as either high or very high, and only two were rated as low: both of the latter were in early programmes. Moreover, 25 of the same 26 sessions were judged to have had a positive atmosphere. This was assisted by the facilitators actively encouraging exchanges between participants and using reflection and open-ended questions, as in the following short exchange:

> *Facilitator:* 'Excellence is a realistic expectation?'
> Participant: 'Yes.'
> *Facilitator:* 'J, you're saying yes.'
> *Facilitator:* 'What do you think, M?'

Programme non-compliance

Observations show that the trainers followed the outline structure of the sessions as presented in the manual. In 33 of the total 47 sessions observed, the manual was followed exactly, and in 14 it was partly followed; the issue is whether there was any perceived threat to programme integrity in the latter 30%. Most of the changes occurred in session 7. In this session, the trainers are told that the focus of the review of what participants have completed in their workbooks should be 'to ensure that offenders have included goals that are clearly directed towards what they will have to deal with to be successful on release' and on helping the offender 'to refine and restate their goals so that they become "SMART" goals'. In the process of setting SMART goals there should be a review of what has been completed in the workbook and the offender should be helped to prioritise and focus, and encouraged to believe in their ability to change. Facilitators are offered a guide, which suggests reference to previous exercises – the puzzle, lifeline, roadblocks, values and the 'miracle' question (what might the individual notice if they woke up one morning and they have reached their desired state) – and it is the lack of specific reference to these that constitutes the changes referred to. However, in all the sessions, the workbook was on the table and constantly referred to; the bullseye (a crucial tool to assist the 'plotting' of goals) was in view and used; and the overall focus of the session was maintained. In some sessions, the offenders put their restated goals on the bullseye and in others the trainer did this for them: the former practice might be seen to enhance a sense of ownership, but this did not appear to be a fundamental issue. Thus, in this respect, no threat to programme integrity was discerned.

Occasionally, facilitators amended the programme in other ways. For example:

* in a session 9, using the script of a film rather than using the film itself;
* in a session 11, reversing the sequence by focusing on responding to success before responding to failure;
* in a session 10, putting a success rating exercise first rather than last;

- in a session 3, describing the seven roadblocks first and then applying the roadblock test (changes that seemed to improve the sessions).

Such amendments, again, were not integrity threatening.

Organisational factors

The conditions in which the groups were run varied in the three prisons, and might reflect differing resource levels in terms of space. There were occasions in one of the prisons when the general requirements of the prison regime seemed to override the needs of the programme; for example, other prison staff would occasionally interrupt groups. However, staff (in each of the prisons) reported an appropriate level of commitment to programme integrity. This is evidenced by the initial input of training by the programme developers (supported by meetings between them and facilitators), and by the mechanisms put in place during the running of the programme itself. Interviews with staff (see Chapter 3) showed that staff across all three sites supported each other with informal feedback following each session, and held regular team meetings. Additionally, treatment managers based in Hull and Parc and the senior facilitator in Lewes reviewed videos of taped sessions and provided constructive feedback to tutors. Moreover, the treatment manager from T3 visited Lewes on several occasions to undertake motivational interviewing training with facilitators and provide feedback on sessions observed.

Concluding comments from observations

'FOR – A Change' is a coherent programme, the structure of which ensures a focus on the core elements of Miller and Rollnick's motivational interviewing model, namely, exploration of ambivalence (aptly explained by the metaphor of the decisional balance) and building motivation to change. Indeed, the single most impressive thing about the programme is the robustness of its design: it facilitates work from participants via different types of facilitator. This is because the required style of directiveness appears to come from the structure and sequence of the programme itself. Of course, there are some design problems and these have been picked up by some of the facilitators, as we see in the next chapter. At times, the process of refining goals seems over-repetitive and some of the concepts are complex; for example, the use of thinking shades is a lot to take in (yet it stands out more than any other exercise for some participants). Moreover, session 13 is written for group delivery and it is stressed that it needs to take place very near to release (difficult to coordinate for a group), and, significantly, some facilitators changed it to an individual session. Indeed, it is interesting that some of the criticisms expressed in the next chapter focus on the programme being simplistic or patronising, because this might on the one hand confirm the programme's coherence but on the other raise questions about the accuracy of matching of treatment to participant (Bernfeld's point about implementation at client level). That said, the programme appears to stimulate participants into meaningful work, probably because it is so clearly focused on the participant's agenda. Generalised aims are refined to specific, personalised goals at the same time as potential impediments to achievement are identified, and, generally, the participants seem to understand both the content and the process.

3

Pre-release interventions: staff and offender perspectives

I n this chapter we explore staff and offender experiences of, and views about, the pre-release stage of the Resettlement Pathfinders, with particular attention to the FOR programme. This includes the experiences of treatment managers, programme tutors and prisoners. Post-release experiences will be discussed in Chapter 4.

Staff perspectives

In addition to frequent informal interaction with them, the evaluation team conducted a total of 24 formal interviews with all the treatment managers and tutors across the three sites. These included five staff members (four of them in Lewes) who were interviewed twice in order to get a clearer picture of progress over time. (A further 13 interviews were conducted with outside probation officers and others linked to FOR who were responsible for the community stage: their views are discussed in Chapter 4.) As well as exploring staff views about the programme in general and their experiences of delivering specific sessions, the semi-structured interview schedule was designed to elicit information relating to a range of practical, organisational and delivery issues. The programme staff were also asked about the nature of other pre-release work carried out with the prisoners and the integration of the FOR programme within the prison, with particular reference to linkage with in-house services.

The following discussion focuses mainly on staff experiences of delivering the programme and their views about its style and content. It is structured under the following headings:

• Comparison with other treatment programmes.
• Session content.
• Programme applicability.
• Workbooks.
• Programme effectiveness and quality of delivery.

Comparison with other treatment programmes

Staff with experience of other prison-based treatment programmes were asked how they thought FOR compared. Staff across all sites were of a similar opinion, in that all those questioned reported that they found the FOR programme exciting and progressive. The flexible format and reliance upon the contribution of participants was thought to distinguish FOR from other programmes currently being run, which tend to be a lot more rigid and structured. As a result of the need to be able to respond spontaneously to and utilise input from participants, tutors found FOR a challenging but professionally fulfilling programme to deliver. Furthermore, the non-directive nature of the programme was cited as one of the reasons why participants seem to engage exceptionally well with the programme and hence why tutors believe it to be so effective:

> 'I think because FOR is non-directive they [the participants] think they have thought of it themselves so they are more likely to do it and that is the best thing about this course. If we let them think they have worked everything out for themselves and they can apply what they have learned to situations they encounter when they are released then you know you have done a good job.'

The practical element incorporated into session 12 near the end of the programme was viewed by staff in all three sites as an extremely positive factor differentiating FOR from other programmes being run within the prison. Staff found, for example, that, although the agency contact in session 12 was not widely publicised by tutors when recruiting prisoners, word of mouth ensured that most were aware of it. It was subsequently thought to be an important consideration for many prisoners when deciding whether or not to join the programme:

> 'I think the best thing about the programme is you can get people in the Marketplace and get them to actually meet people and book appointments and know that when they go out they have that waiting for them and they aren't just walking out of the gate.'

> 'When I compare FOR to STOP [Straight Thinking on Probation], for example, I like FOR better. FOR allows for a certain degree of innovation and creativity. It is shorter, punchier and it contains that practical element at the end that no other course does and those are the big differences for me.'

Nevertheless, the staff at Lewes had some reservations about the efficacy of the Marketplace session and thought that it was delivered too late in the programme. This could be attributable to the lack of service providers in the East Sussex area, combined with poor commitment of local agencies to the programme. In response to this, an additional Marketplace session was made available to inmates participating in the programme. Although all the inmates attended the Marketplace at session 12, most of them had been given the opportunity to attend before this point:

'They just get an additional one, a chance for them to come along and see how it works and see that within the programme there are other things building.'

Session content

When asked their opinions about session content, staff in all three sites were mainly positive. They thought the programme generally worked well, was pitched at an appropriate level and engaged participants. However, staff in Lewes felt that parts of the programme needed to be simplified and broken down in order for the majority of offenders to understand:

'It's a tough course, it is a lot to take in, some of the sessions unless you do break them down I think a lot of people do struggle to take the information in ... I think you've got to realise that the people you're working with, not all of them but a few, haven't had the best education and you've got to bring it down to their level rather than bring it up to that level, high level.'

In addition, it was stated by several interviewees that they had had to adapt some of the written exercises for prisoners with poor writing skills. In such instances, other techniques were used, such as bullet points or storyboarding, which the clients could then expand upon during the group discussion or in the one-to-one session.

The participant-centred focus of the programme was thought to be a particularly effective method of helping offenders to internalise the goals of each session as the examples and scenarios used were highly relevant:

'I think FOR is all the best bits of R&R [a full-length cognitive-behavioural programme] condensed and made into a very punchy programme. It is so real for them; it appeals to their egocentricity, which gets them buying. You are talking about the thing most important to them which is themselves and their life when they get out. I love the theory side of it because it works and putting that together with the practicalities of it is a superb combination.'

Nonetheless, some staff in Lewes and Parc felt that parts of the programme were 'too long-winded and repetitive', especially the tasks relating to goal setting around session 7. Consequently, these staff disagreed with the programme authors' view that expressions of apathy or boredom from participants were signs of resistance: rather, they felt they resulted from the style and structure of particular sessions:

'I find around session 7 it becomes very repetitive around targets and goals and people seem to, you know, find it difficult to continuously reset, re-evaluate, reset, and re-evaluate, reset.'

'I know the facilitators say that people saying "you are going over this again and again" is resistance to change. I'm not so sure, I think it's simply that they can't see the point of it, you keep sifting it and getting the same result.'

'I think when we do the first and second cut of the goals, if we've really explained it well to them they've already gone to the second cut. They know exactly what they need to do, what they don't need to do and there isn't a need for a cut.'

The commitment matrix used in session 8 to develop the personal change plan was highlighted as a particularly challenging concept for participants to understand. Several staff reported that they tended to lose participants' attention during this task. One tutor also expressed concerns that participants were getting confused while completing the commitment matrix in this session. For example, the manual states that individuals must commit to a goal because they 'want to' and not because they feel they 'ought to'. However, some participants felt that the two were not mutually exclusive.

Programme applicability

In the second phase Pathfinders, amendments to the eligibility criteria meant that young offenders (YOs) were able to join the programme. In view of this, staff were asked how appropriate they thought the programme was to this group of prisoners. Interviewees in Parc generally thought that the inclusion of YOs within the programme had improved the group dynamics. Tutors observed that a two-way learning process seemed to operate between the adults and the younger participants, whereby the adults tempered their behaviour and adopted an advisory role, while the YOs showed enthusiasm and a willingness to learn that may not have been so apparent in older prisoners:

'What is interesting is you get the adults saying look you are going to end up like me and the YOs say to them we have lessons for you too with our enthusiasm and unspoiled ability to make progress. I think the programme is applicable to any age.'

Despite initial reservations, staff in Hull also found that the programme worked well with a mixed group of YOs and adult offenders. An attempt was made to run the programme with a group comprised solely of YOs, but the programme was postponed after only one session due to staff illness. Although Lewes does not have a YO population, the FOR team felt that the programme would be applicable to this group. Nevertheless, staff across all three sites felt that certain aspects of the programme (such as the use of a 'timeline' in session 2) should be altered for groups comprised only of YOs.

Workbooks

Some tutors in Parc expressed minor concerns about aspects of the workbook. It was queried, in particular, whether it would be suitable for female participants, as all examples and scenarios relate to men. Additionally, one tutor thought there may be a problem stemming from the cultural disparity between the Americanised language used throughout the manual and workbooks and the language used by participants in South Wales:

'There are parts of FOR that probably are not culturally right for the people we deal with in South Wales. Odd things come up, some things are Americanised such as the moral dilemma examples like: you are working in a movie theatre.'

Further, doubts were expressed as to the suitability of some of the graphics used throughout the workbook. Some tutors felt they were too childish and could be interpreted as patronising by the participants:

'You have a bunch of guys here, a lot of them are hardened cons and the book has pictures of crayons. It might be alright for the YOs but not for the adults and some of the guys who do this programme are intelligent people with degrees and professional qualifications and a little picture of crayons doesn't go down too well.'

Nonetheless, the workbooks were being used effectively and found to be helpful to both the inmates and the staff in all three sites:

'I think the majority seem to think they're really good and they're really proud of them and yes they do the work step by step in the book.'

Programme effectiveness and quality of delivery

When asked what they thought were the key aims and objectives of the FOR programme, staff in all sites tended to emphasise the need to address cognitive deficits underlying offending behaviour, while at the same time building prisoners' motivation and confidence to pursue their goals and tackle practical problems for themselves on release. In view of the association made by the programme between cognitive and practical problems, help linking up with community-based agencies to aid the transition from custody to community was also seen as vital. Typical responses included:

'It is more than about helping them change, it is about giving people the confidence and ability to take control of their lives back … to feel that they are better equipped and can deal with inevitable setbacks in areas such as their relationships and addictions.'

'It's for people to identify first and foremost their needs and offending behaviours to become motivated through their own awareness and identifying that themselves without being told you know, and for them to be able to set out a way of getting out of that behaviour pattern but all coming from their own agendas and identifying that and becoming aware of the cycle they are in.'

Reflecting findings from the observational study (Chapter 2), tutors in Lewes agreed that they had become far more familiar with the programme material over the past six months and consequently were able to deliver the sessions with greater confidence. This could, in part, have been attributable to the increased amount of in-house training received by tutors and feedback provided by the T3 treatment manager following her visits to Lewes, as well as more opportunity to facilitate in groups:

'I have a lot more confidence, more relaxed. I can hop in and out of the programme and don't need to follow it quite as religiously as I did. I still make sure everything is done but don't need to read it word verbatim.'

'I feel my teaching style has become more snappy, more direct; rather than taking five-and-a-half minutes to get the point it's two minutes. Focusing on the essence of something and getting it out quite quickly.'

Moreover, a post-release tutor in Brighton was certain that there had been an improvement in the delivery of the pre-release phase of the programme, as she had perceived a positive change in FOR participants after release:

'I think the programme has become a lot more organised and I think the delivery has improved, going on the way that the clients present in the first session. It has been a big learning curve for all of us.'

Conversely, however, a staff member in Parc commented that the increased number of programmes being run by the unit, combined with a degree of staleness and complacency after running FOR for a long period, had negatively affected some tutors' delivery of FOR:

'So many tutors are now involved with other programmes that they haven't got the focus that they used to have on it. The newer tutors are a lot more focused and conscientious about the delivery than some older tutors are. Tutors need pass or fail training so people know it matters and work hard at it, there needs to be pressure. It is too easy otherwise; there just isn't the discipline.'

Finally, it was generally believed by staff in all sites that the pre-release phase of the programme was successfully meeting the objective of motivating participants to address their offending behaviour. However, it was also felt that much of the progress made prior to release was being undermined by poor community service provision in all three areas:

> 'I think we're getting the point across of the programme but virtually 100% of them will say "Well that's all very well but what real help is there for me to actually change this?" There is very little actual help here. I mean if you can actually get someone going out with no fixed abode if you could actually get them accommodation then I think you'd feel that you'd achieved something. But you're going through this process and they're saying this is my problem and there is very little we can do to actually help them.'

Offender perspectives

We now turn to the views and experiences of offenders who participated in the projects, again in relation to the pre-release phase of the programme, and particularly the FOR programme. The analysis is based on 163 interviews conducted with participants while they were still in custody and a further 71 interviews with those among them who could be located and were willing to be interviewed after release (their perspectives on the post-release stage is discussed in Chapter 4). It was aimed to interview a minimum of 50 participants in each prison who had completed a minimum of six programme sessions and were still in custody at the time of our research visits. Every prisoner who met these criteria was interviewed until the quotas were exceeded, and none of those approached for interview refused: they can therefore be regarded as constituting a broadly representative sample of all those who remained on the programme beyond the halfway point. By contrast, it is likely that the 71 among them who were interviewed post-release constituted a somewhat 'skewed' sample, in that, by dint of being relatively easy to contact and keeping the interview appointments, they were as a group probably more settled and more positive towards the programme and its aims than those we failed to locate and/or interview.

Reasons for joining and perceived benefits

The 163 FOR participants interviewed in custody were first asked why they had decided to join the programme and what they thought it could help them with. As Figure 3.1 shows, almost a third named 'help staying out of trouble' as their principal reason, while 22% wanted help with drug or alcohol problems. 'Curiosity' was cited as the main reason for joining by 11%, help with accommodation by 9% and an opportunity to 'get out of the cell' also by 9%. Only 4% reported joining the programme to get help with education or employment.

Figure 3.1: Principal reasons for joining the FOR programme

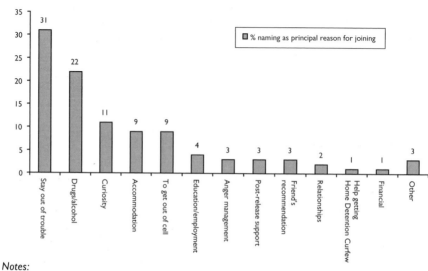

Notes:

n = 163.

Percentages do not total 100 due to rounding.

When asked what they thought they had most gained by participating, more than half (52%) cited improved thinking skills. Fourteen per cent felt that the programme had given them a sense of direction and goals to aim for in life, while 10% thought they had achieved greater self-confidence. One offender felt for example that, 'FOR has given me a lot of confidence and belief in myself that I can change, I didn't have that before'. Another commented: 'I now look at life differently, it has pointed me in the right direction, linked me up with outside agencies and changed the way I think about things. I'll try to stop coming back to jail'.

A further gain mentioned by 6% of participants was *learning* where to ask for help in the future. Very few believed that help with practical problems was the main benefit of FOR; and only 1% thought the programme had helped with drug or accommodation problems.

Conversely, 9% of those interviewed felt that the programme had not helped them at all. Five claimed that the programme focused too much on 'school work' and had failed to help them with their practical needs, notably, lack of accommodation. Two felt that, as they had no major problems, the programme was not relevant to them, and four participants merely commented that they had found it interesting as opposed to helpful. One participant said that it 'skimmed over things too much and needed to be more in-depth', while another thought that the programme was too repetitive. Finally, one offender had wanted help with anger management, which he thought the programme did not provide.

Participants were also asked to identify which session had been the most important to them. Just over a quarter (26%) could not identify one particular session as being more important than the others. Of those who could, 20% named session 4 (the six shades of thinking). The sessions focusing on participants' goals (6 and 8) also stood out for a significant proportion (18%). Interestingly, while almost a quarter (22%) claimed to have joined the programme to access drug or alcohol services, only 9% said that the Marketplace session (12) had been the most important to them.

Retrospective views

As noted earlier, 71 of the 163 offenders interviewed in prison were contacted and reinterviewed post-release. In nearly all cases, these interviews were conducted between one and three months after release. It is re-emphasised that these 71 cannot be regarded as representative of all ex-prisoners who had participated in the FOR programme, because those we were unable to contact, or who failed to keep interview appointments, are likely to have been less settled and less positively disposed towards the programme than those who were found and interviewed.

While most of this second interview focused on post-release issues, respondents were also asked to think back to the programme and consider, with hindsight, which specific aspects of it had been most helpful to them. Table 3.1 provides a breakdown of their responses.

It can be seen that only six of the 71 were unable to recall any specific aspects that had been useful to them. Of the 65 individuals who could do so, much higher numbers mentioned improved cognitive abilities and/or emotional support than more practical forms of help. For example, 28 mentioned the 'six shades of thinking' as the most helpful, many of these commenting that they had improved their ability to think before acting. Thirteen participants reported that understanding of the need to plan ahead and set goals had been of particular assistance to them, and a further seven highlighted the ability to problem solve and develop alternative thinking. The more 'practical' benefit of contact with service agencies was mentioned as one of the most helpful aspects by just seven respondents. Perhaps surprisingly, given the focus of the programme, only two mentioned motivation specifically.

Table 3.1: Aspects of FOR programme recalled by ex-prisoners as of most help

	Number	%
Thinking before acting – using shades	28	39
Setting goals and planning ahead	13	18
Alternative thinking and problem-solving skills	7	10
Contact with service agencies	7	10
Learning past mistakes – roadblocks	3	4
Improved confidence in own abilities	3	4
Increased motivation	2	3
Thinking of other people's feelings	1	1
Looking at past – timeline and my story	1	1
Nothing specific stands out	6	9
Total	71	100

Referrals to other services

FOR participants interviewed before their release were asked whether they had yet been referred to any other service agencies, based inside or outside prison (including appointments to be taken up after release). Overall, 48% of the 163 interviewed had been so referred. However, if only those prisoners who had already attended session 12 – the Marketplace – are selected, the proportion referred to at least one agency rises to almost three quarters (69 out of 95). Table 3.2 shows the types of services concerned. Nearly 40% of the 95 who attended session 12 had been referred to employment agencies, and over a quarter to accommodation services. A similar proportion had been referred to external drugs agencies. CARATS, the prison-based drugs service, received about half this number of referrals from among the session 12 attendees.[1]

It is also important to acknowledge that while session 12 – the Marketplace – serves as the principal means of linking FOR participants with local agencies, nine individuals reported that they had been referred on to services prior to this point in the programme.

---

[1] CARATS stands for Counselling, Advice, Referral, Assessment and Throughcare Services.

Table 3.2: Types of referrals made in session 12 of the FOR programme

Type of service referred to	% of session 12 attendees referred to an agency (n = 95)
Employment	39
Drug	26
Accommodation	26
CARATS	14
FOR community link	6
Alcohol	4
Counselling	3
Financial/benefits advice	3
Other	8
Any agency	73

Notes:
Full sample n = 163.
Members of sample attending session 12 = 95.
Total of session attendees referred to at least one agency = 69.
Interviewees could give more than one response.

Participants were also asked whether they had received any help during their sentence from services not linked to the FOR programme. Fifty-eight reported having received such help. Table 3.3 presents a breakdown of the type of help received in each prison. Just under half (46%) of the participants interviewed in Parc had received help from sources other than FOR, compared with 21% at Lewes and 35% in Hull. This help was typically from CARATS workers and in-prison careers services.

Expectations of contact after release

Of the 81 Automatic Unconditional Release (AUR) participants interviewed pre-release, almost three quarters (72%) wished to remain in contact with the FOR team following their release from prison. These 58 respondents were asked to give reasons for this, and what they hoped to gain from voluntary contact or supervision. Table 3.4 presents a breakdown of the principal reasons given. 'Having someone to talk to' or 'general support with problems' (20/58) and 'help staying off drugs/ alcohol' (11/58) were the most commonly cited reasons.

Table 3.3: Help received from sources other than FOR (numbers)

	Parc	Lewes	Hull	Total
CARATs worker	8	8	7	23
Counsellor	4	0	0	4
In-prison careers service	3	2	6	11
In-prison drug course	4	0	1	5
In-prison accommodation service	3	0	3	6
Wing officers	4	0	0	4
External careers service	3	0	2	5
External accommodation service	2	1	0	3
Benefits advice	0	0	3	3
External drug agency	2	0	3	5
No additional help received	35	34	36	105
Total number of responses	68	45	61	174

Note:
Number of cases = 163, number of responses = 174. Respondents could give more than one response.

Table 3.4: Main reason for wishing to maintain post-release contact

Reason for wanting post-release contact	Number	%
To have someone to talk to/general support with problems	20	35
Stay off drugs/alcohol	11	19
Continuity – tutors already known to participants (Hull and Lewes only)	9	16
Help with accommodation	7	12
Help with employment/education	5	9
Reminder of programme/goals	2	3
Help with finances/benefits	1	2
Other	3	5
Total	58	101

Note:
n = 58. Percentages do not total 100 due to rounding.

A clear majority (86%) of the 58 AUR prisoners who wished to remain in contact felt that the programme had effected a positive change in their attitudes towards help or guidance that might be offered by probation or other post-release services. One commented:

'I now look at probation as a bonus, more help has given me more determination to better myself, FOR has changed my whole outlook on life.'

Even those subject to mandatory licences tended to feel more positive about their coming supervision. Of the 69 Automatic Conditional Release (ACR) prisoners interviewed, 48 (70%) said that the programme had made them more positive about this. One ACR prisoner revealed, for example, that:

'If I hadn't done FOR I would have breached my probation and wouldn't have seen it as a help. Now I know the probation officer, she knows my problems and my goals. I'd rather see the FOR PO [probation officer] than a stranger and I'll show her my workbook.'

This last comment underlines the importance of FOR community links visiting participants prior to their release from prison, in order to boost continuity and develop rapport.

Criticisms of the programme

Finally, participants were asked if they had any criticisms of the programme or any suggestions for improvement. Fifty-eight of the 163 interviewed pre-release proposed changes to the programme, with the remaining 105 satisfied with it in its current state. Table 3.5 provides a breakdown of respondents' criticisms and suggestions.

Lack of help with practical issues such as housing, drugs and employment was the kind of criticism expressed most frequently. It was also said on several occasions that the practical help offered in session 12, the Marketplace, should be made available earlier in the programme. For example:

'It needs to include more help with accommodation, need something more concrete, because I know all my goals will fall in to place if I get somewhere to live.'

'It would be better if we got to see agencies at a much earlier stage rather than just session 12. Think it is a very good thing that housing and probation are in the same room; they know who you've seen and can't fob you off.'

'I would like more practical help throughout, as I can't be here for the last session anyway because I'm released the day before....'

On a related topic, six participants felt that the agencies that attended the Marketplace needed to cover a much wider geographic area. One of these commented:

Table 3.5: Offenders' criticisms of and suggestions for improvement to the FOR programme

Criticism	Number
More practical help with housing/drugs/employment	10
More one-to-one work	7
Have less gaps between sessions/more consistency[a]	6
Have agencies in session 12 covering a wider area	6
Have more in-depth/longer sessions	5
Have less written work	4
Exclude the shades session	4
Programme is too repetitive	4
Improve assessment procedures (exclude time-wasters, etc)	4
Programme too patronising – pitch it at a higher level	3
Too much like school	3
Wing staff need to be more informed about FOR	2
Show a different film	2
Programme focuses on the past too much	2
Other[b]	5
No criticisms	105
Total number of responses[c]	172

Notes:
[a] Lewes only.
[b] 'Other' includes 'have closer links with drug rehab services' (1), 'have a greater focus on needs of participants' families' (1), 'scrap all homework' (1), 'offer programme to DCRs' (ie prisoners serving more than 4 years) (1), 'have a longer icebreaker session at the outset' (1).
[c] Number of cases = 163, number of responses = 172. Interviewees could give more than one response.

'Think there needed to be a wider variety of housing officers from different areas. Maybe have a counsellor there.'

Seven claimed that they would have preferred more one-to-one sessions in which they could look into aspects of their offending behaviour and life history that they did not feel able to discuss within a group setting. For example:

'I would have liked more one-to-one sessions, especially on life story. I didn't think the session was appropriate in a group situation.'

'I would have liked to do more one-to-one work rather than group work. I don't want other people that I don't know knowing my past.'

Finally, there were also a few criticisms concerning organisational arrangements, including references to occasions when programme sessions had to be cancelled due to lack of staffing, and poor communication between landing officers and FOR staff:

'I think it should have been better organised, sometimes waiting around, not knowing if there is a group or not, there needs to be more communication between officers on the landings and programme staff so we don't miss out on anything.'

Post-release contact and services

4

I n this chapter, the focus is upon post-release aspects of the resettlement process. The discussion is based on four main data sources: the interviews – already referred to in the previous chapter – with 71 ex-prisoners who had previously completed the FOR programme; interviews with 13 FOR 'community links' or 'post-release tutors'; a postal questionnaire completed by 24 community-based service providers with links to the programme; and analysis of the post-release sections of the case management records (CMRs) kept on all FOR participants.

First, a brief summary is given of the extent of contact between offenders and FOR staff or community links: this issue is further discussed in Chapter 5, where post-release contact is examined as an interim indicator of resettlement outcomes. Second, an account is given of referrals made to local agencies and of subsequent levels of service uptake. Finally, views of the community link staff and ex-prisoners are presented.

Post-release contact with the project teams

It is important to reiterate that the evaluation of the Phase 1 Resettlement Pathfinders included only Automatic Unconditional Release (AUR) prisoners (for whom all post-release contact was voluntary), but that the eligibility criteria were expanded in Phase 2 to include Automatic Conditional Release (ACR) prisoners and young offenders (YOs), two groups that are subject to statutory post-release supervision. This complicated the post-release stages of the resettlement strategy, which were managed differently in each site.

As outlined in Chapter 1, the aim in Parc was to allocate all ACR participants to specially designated (and trained) FOR probation officers in a number of locations around South Wales: while this occurred in most cases, a substantial minority were in fact supervised by other members of throughcare teams. In Hull and Lewes, ACR participants served their licence with their originally allocated probation officer and were able to contact members of the FOR teams as an additional support mechanism if they wished. In Hull, too, it will be remembered, it was built into the project plan from the outset that the prison-based team would also be responsible for a significant amount of post-release work.

It should be noted that efforts to maintain contact on a voluntary basis with AUR prisoners could take a variety of forms, including telephone calls and reminder letters from staff to prisoners. However, the statistics on 'contact' in this chapter focus upon face-to-face contact only. Attempts were made to measure other forms of contact, but the data produced by the projects were not sufficiently reliable, due to poor recording practices. Additionally, it is believed that by measuring face-to-face contact only, a more accurate reflection of participants' motivation to maintain meaningful contact is obtained.

At the time we 'closed the books' on the evaluation, 250 of the 278 prisoners who had completed the FOR programme had been released. According to the case records, some face-to-face contact was made after release between FOR staff (or designated FOR links) and at least 109 (44%) of these 250 prisoners. About 65% of the ACR completers, 55% of the YO completers and 28% of AUR completers had such contact (see Table 4.1).

Table 4.1: Post-release face-to-face contact between ex-prisoners and FOR staff/links: released programme completers only

	AUR		ACR		YO		Total	
Site	%	Number	%	Number	%	Number	%	Number
Parc	19	9/47	72	31/43	55	11/20	46	51/110
Hull	45	23/51	70	14/20	56	5/9	52	42/80
Lewes	17	7/40	45	9/20	0	0	27	16/60
All sites	28	39/138	65	54/83	55	16/29	44	109/250

Of the three sites, Hull achieved by far the highest rate of contact with released short-termers who had completed FOR (45%). By contrast, Parc's AUR contact rate was lower than it had been in Phase 1, suggesting that the new system whereby particular probation officers were trained and designated as 'FOR links' did not work very well with short-termers. On the other hand, rates of contact between FOR links and ACR prisoners were greater in Parc than elsewhere, because these officers were often given the primary responsibility for statutory supervision.

Table 4.2 outlines the numbers of face-to-face contacts recorded in respect of the 138 released AUR prisoners who had completed FOR. It indicates that, although a substantial proportion of participants from Hull made some post-release contact with members of the FOR team, more than half of these saw them only once. Across the three sites, indeed, only four AUR completers were seen more than six times by project staff.[1]

---

[1] One of these was in voluntary face-to-face contact with Lewes community links at least 12 times. Lewes also saw numerous times an ex-prisoner who had not completed the programme.

**Table 4.2: Numbers of face-to-face contacts post-release with AUR
participants, by site: released AUR programme completers only (%)**

Site	No contact	1	2-3	4-6	7-10	11+	Total
Parc	81	13	2	4	–	–	100 (n = 47)
Hull	55	24	14	2	6	–	101 (n = 51)
Lewes	83	10	–	5	–	2	100 (n = 40)
All sites	72	16	6	4	2	1	101 (n = 138)

Note:
Percentages do not always total 100 due to rounding.

Referrals and service uptake

We now look in more detail at the 'referrals' of prisoners and ex-prisoners made by
the FOR teams in each site, and at levels of service uptake post-release. The term
'referral' is somewhat vague and is interpreted in many different ways by service
agencies. Staff in the three sites used it variously to include providing information,
suggesting that an offender contacts a given agency and setting up an appointment
on an offender's behalf. Moreover, while many 'referrals' did not result in any
contact with the agency concerned, there were also occasions on which staff visited
the agencies with participants in order to ensure that appointments were kept.
In this study, we have attempted to separate 'referrals' that consisted essentially
of providing offenders with information (for example, giving them the telephone
number of, or a leaflet about, a particular agency) from referrals of a more concrete
and proactive nature, which include or lead to the making of at least a provisional
appointment. The latter kinds of referral could be made during the Marketplace
session or as part of post-release work.

Kept appointments

Table 4.3 provides a breakdown of 'successful' referrals made through the
Pathfinder teams or their link staff, or self-referrals made by prisoners themselves
at the Marketplace session, in the sense of appointments resulting in attendance
at external service agencies. Although probably distorted to some extent by
incomplete record-keeping, the figures provide a broad sense of the shape of post-
release contact with other agencies. Altogether, at least 82 appointments were kept
(by 65 individuals). Assistance with accommodation was clearly the most common
service accessed by ex-prisoners from Parc and Lewes, although not in Hull (where
housing was relatively cheap and available). Otherwise, employment and drugs
agencies were the most frequently contacted. It should also be noted that at least
15 applications were made, with staff help, for places on educational or training
courses.

Table 4.3: Numbers of referrals resulting in kept appointments, post-release: all released prisoners who had started FOR (n = 311)

Type of referral	Parc	Lewes	Hull	All
Referred to and attended accommodation service	17	9	5	31
Referred to and attended employment service	11	2	6	19
Referred to and attended drugs agency	5	5	8	18
Referred to and attended alcohol agency	3	2	1	6
Referred to and attended counselling	5	2	1	8

The case management records (CMRs) were also examined for evidence of the outcomes of these referrals and kept appointments. It was clear that at least seven individuals eventually obtained accommodation as a result of the assistance offered, at least eight found employment and at least eight were able to get onto college/training courses. These figures are likely to be underestimates, due to missing data.

Further relevant evidence is available from the interview data. Among the 71 participants interviewed post-release, 43 (61%) reported having been referred through the FOR teams or their community links to an external agency. Of these 43, 16 reported that they had failed to attend their appointments, and had not contacted the agency since. The other 27 had contacted the agency concerned. In turn, 19 of these 27 had received some help, the remaining eight claiming that the agency had been unable to help them.

Perspectives from community service providers

Further information about post-release services and their take-up levels can be gleaned from the results of telephone interviews with members of 24 community agencies which had regular links with the FOR programme, principally through attendance at the Marketplace session at each site. These comprised three agencies from Hull, 11 from the Brighton area and 10 from South Wales. All but one of those contacted agreed to an interview. Questions were asked about service provision, procedures for clients getting accepted into the agency, the nature and extent of contact with the FOR programme and agency workers' opinions of the usefulness and effectiveness of FOR.

It should be noted that the Marketplace operated differently in Hull to the other two prisons. In Parc and Lewes, representatives from the same 10 or 11 agencies were invited to the session every time, enabling prisoners to discuss their resettlement needs directly, obtain advice and make appointments for release. However, referrals to community services in Hull were made either through the Counselling, Advice, Referral, Assessment and Throughcare services (CARATs) team or via the prison's in-house referral service and thus community agencies had very little direct contact with the FOR programme. Consequently, only three services were included in the Hull sample as they were the only agencies within the area to have been in direct contact with the FOR programme team.

Table 4.4 provides a description of the 24 agencies which were linked directly with the FOR programmes. It shows that all but five were voluntary. Of the five statutory services, four dealt with employment, education and training, while the fifth was a general support and advice service. Indeed, another seven of the 19 voluntary agencies provided assistance with employment, education and training; six dealt with drug or alcohol abuse; and three helped with accommodation.

Table 4.4: Descriptive overview of services linked with the FOR programme

	%	Number
Type of service		
Statutory	21	5/24
Voluntary	79	20/24
Agency capacity		
<10	8	2/24
10-20	4	1/24
21-100	38	9/24
101-500	25	6/24
501-1,000	8	2/24
>1,000	8	2/24
Don't know	8	2/24
Service provision		
Employment/education/training	46	11/24
Drugs/alcohol	25	6/24
General advice/mentoring	17	4/24
Accommodation	13	3/24
Waiting time for access to services		
< 1 week	38	9/24
1-2 weeks	21	5/24
3-4 weeks	8	2/24
> 2 months	4	1/24
Other	29	7/24

Waiting times for access to services were said by the agencies to be relatively short. Over a third reported a waiting time of less than a week and a fifth between one and two weeks. Clients had to wait more than two months to receive treatment at only one agency.

All but two agencies reported having had direct contact with the FOR programme, mainly through the Marketplace sessions. However, exchange of information was fairly low outside these sessions. Only five respondents reported that their agency had received literature from the programme, five that they had been visited by FOR programme staff and five that the FOR team checked with them regarding client attendance. Moreover, only four reported that FOR and agency staff attended joint meetings.

Respondents were asked how many clients had been referred to their agency in the past year via the FOR programme. Ten were unable to provide this information. Six of the 14 who could reported that they had received more than 10 referrals, and a further five that they had received more than five. The questionnaire also asked how many of these referrals had led to ex-prisoners from the FOR programme attending at least one appointment. Only one agency reported visits from more than 10 offenders: most saw between one and five, and five saw none at all.

Respondents were presented with a scale of 1 to 5, where 1 represented 'very good' and 5 'very poor', and asked to select which best described their working relationship with the FOR scheme. Respondents in South Wales were most likely to answer 'very good', with six of the 10 agencies feeling this way, compared with three of the 11 in the Brighton area. Two of the three Hull agencies reported that they had not experienced enough direct contact with the programme to comment. Only one agency anywhere reported having a 'very bad' relationship with a Pathfinder project.

Finally, the community agency respondents were asked about their general perceptions and opinions of the FOR programme. First of all, when asked, using a similar five-point scale, how useful they thought it was to have a prison-based resettlement programme targeting cognitive-motivational deficits in addition to practical needs, all but one rated this approach as very or fairly useful. Second, when asked for any other general comments, including criticisms and suggestions for improvement, the most frequent response concerned the need for more contact between the FOR teams and the agencies (see Table 4.5). Several also made critical comments about the organisation of the Marketplace, especially in relation to mismatches between their catchment areas and the areas to which the prisoners were being released.

Table 4.5: Agency representatives' general comments about the FOR programme

Issue referred to	Number mentioning
Need more multi-agency contact/more contact with FOR staff/ better communication	11
Marketplace is poorly run/not enough offenders released to agency catchment area	8
Agencies need more pre-release contact with participants/ Marketplace is too little too late	4
Favourable comments: improves multi-agency work/clients speak highly of it/improves motivation/reduces re-offending, etc	9
Funding and continuity difficulties	1

Note:
Numbers do not total to 24 as respondents could give more than one response.

Perspectives of post-release tutors

The main role of the 'post-release tutors' (or 'community links' as they were often called) was envisaged by the programme designers as to enhance the offenders' motivation to achieve the goals and aims that they had set during the custody stage of FOR. Although they differed somewhat on the extent to which they thought they should also assist offenders with practical problems, the key motivational role was recognised by all 13 of the post-release tutors interviewed. For example:

> 'My role is to keep up the motivation when the clients come into the community and to identify the goals. I think for the clients it changes on release and I think my job is to re-identify the goals for the clients on release and to look at whether they need to be readjusted.'

While the post-release tutors were extremely supportive of the programme, they reported a number of problems, which hindered their work. These were fairly specific to each of the three sites.

In Parc, their role within probation was said by all those interviewed to have conflicted with their role as a FOR tutor. It was generally felt that they had received very little recognition from the probation service of their FOR work. This led to problems of increased caseloads, lack of time to dedicate to the FOR programme and a sense of isolation and marginalisation:

> 'There is little support, no one here has the time or the inclination to be interested in FOR, so it's left to me, I'm responsible for it and I am on my own here.... It is not a criticism of the staff here, it is a criticism of the organisation, that it hasn't got the resources or isn't inclined to give it.'

'We [the community tutors] don't communicate at all, the only time we communicate is when we see each other at the Marketplace.... I do feel that the post-release phase of the programme is marginalised to a certain extent, as there is no real support for us in the community. We are all on our own out in our areas and we are not sure if what we are doing is right.'

The post-release tutors, however, did not put any blame for the situation on the prison staff, who were felt to be extremely supportive:

'The relationship with the prison is excellent. It can cause problems when you have two separate yet interlinked agencies trying to work together, but I have found them very welcoming, we are made to feel a part of the whole programme.'

Some similar problems with probation were reported by the Lewes community link seconded from the probation service. More generally, however, the Lewes interviews reflected concerns about a certain lack of communication and support among the FOR team itself. While information was being communicated to the relevant parties, some post-release tutors felt that they would have benefited from more formal meetings:

'I think a monthly meeting would be a good idea to iron out the creases. I would benefit from getting feedback from tutors with regard to how clients have done on the group. I would also put more focus on the programme, because at times when there has been periods when there hasn't been any clients, it's not until you actually get a referral that you get your FOR head back on. If we had monthly meetings we would have kept that focus a bit more.'

In addition, some of the post-release tutors at HMP Lewes stated that they had problems with FOR client allocation, especially in relation to ACR prisoners. This again was attributed to lack of communication:

'I felt that probation were being quite protective over their caseloads ... basically they didn't want them working with me, that's the way it came across.'

At HMP Hull, the FOR tutors handled the post-release stages of the programme themselves. Very few problems were expressed, and most felt that this system worked well, increasing the likelihood that offenders would contact them post-release:

'We maintain a relationship from the first moment we see people on the first contact and maintain that right the way through to the post-release phase. We have realised the importance of this and that they are happier coming to see people that they have dealt with.'

Overall, the post-release tutors in all three sites felt that the programme had a positive effect on offenders. Indeed, a number of post-release tutors commented that FOR participants were noticeably more focused and motivated than their non-FOR clients. For example:

> 'People that have done the programme, people who I've known before they went into prison and did the programme, there is a dramatic change in them when they come out, a positive change in people. They are more focused and more likely to turn up for appointments. They are more likely to seek a solution, an independent solution as well.'

Perspectives of FOR participants

A final perspective on post-release contact and services can be obtained from analysis of the post-release interviews we conducted with FOR participants themselves. Among the 71 interviewed, 47 had made some post-release contact with a FOR tutor/community link: these comprised 12 of the 30 AUR prisoners interviewed, and 35 of the 41 ACR prisoners and YOs.[2]

Of the 47 who had made post-release contact, the majority viewed the experience positively and seemed reassured by knowing the extra support was there for them, 'just in case'. Many saw the provision of post-release support as a continuation of the FOR programme and felt that the regular progress reviews of the goals set while in prison increased their motivation to stay crime-free:

> 'I find meeting [the community support worker] helpful because he looks back at the stuff I did in prison about my goals and aims and stuff, he helps keep me on track.'

> 'Contact with FOR community staff has been good and is better than seeing probation, I saw them the first day I got out and needed someone to talk to. [They are there] if I'm feeling down and need advice.'

Further, the ability of community FOR staff to help with more practical problems such as homelessness and unemployment was also viewed as a major benefit of maintaining post-release contact with FOR staff:

> 'I drop in now and again without an appointment, I need that extra support for a chat and to help with housing problems and stuff like that.'

---

[2] As one would expect, these 'contact rates' are higher than those of the sample as a whole, as the more contact participants had with post-release tutors, the more likely they were to be available and willing to be interviewed.

'They have given me lots of help and advice about grants and benefits and made an appointment for me to speak to someone about my finances.'

However, there were some dissenting voices. Notably, ACR participants in South Wales completing their licence under the supervision of FOR-trained probation officers had mixed views about the post-release phase of the programme. On the one hand, some felt that FOR-trained officers were more supportive and helpful than the probation officers who had supervised them in the past and thus felt more positive about successfully completing their licence:

'I feel my licence is a continuation of FOR, the work is more structured than with the other probation officer, setting goals and giving me encouragement and he [the FOR-trained probation officer] thinks I am doing okay.'

'They have been really helpful and positive. I see my probation officer all the time and come in voluntarily to see him even when I haven't got an appointment to ask his advice as much as possible.'

On the other hand, others had more negative perceptions of probation and felt that the potential benefits of the post-release stage of the programme were undermined by the involvement of the probation service. Indeed, several individuals commented that they would have preferred the opportunity to meet with the programme tutors from the prison post-release instead of probation officers:

'I would never turn down help but it would have been nice to have seen the tutors instead of probation as probation do nothing.'

'I don't want to see more of probation than I have to. It makes no difference that they have been trained in FOR, they are still probation officers.'

Finally, Table 4.6 provides a breakdown of the reasons given by the 18 AUR prisoners who had not contacted their FOR link on release. The majority claimed that they did not need any help, that no help would be forthcoming or simply that they had not had time.

Table 4.6: Reasons given by AUR participants for not contacting FOR team on release

Reason	Number
Haven't needed help	8
Didn't think probation could help	3
Haven't had time	3
Seeing a CARATS worker instead	1
Relapsed on drugs	1
Haven't been able to contact them	1
Re-offended – been in prison since	1
Total	18

5

Impact and outcome measures

Conclusions about the impact on offenders of participation in the second stage Pathfinders are limited by the fact that the available resources did not permit us to collect similar data on a valid comparison group of non-participants. The only comparison groups used in the evaluation were constructed during Phase 1 in order to support a reconviction study, the first (one-year) results of which are presented briefly later in this chapter.

Nevertheless, some useful indications of the impact of the programme in Phase 2 can be obtained from the data collected on participants. In the first part of the chapter we focus on three 'proxy' measures of effectiveness. The first of these is 'continuity of service', which is defined as the proportion of participants who remained in contact with the FOR programme team (or its community links) beyond their day of release. This was chosen because a central concern of all resettlement services is to promote service uptake after release; this was also a key aim of all three projects. The second and third measures relate to changes in participants' attitudes to crime and in their perceived 'life problems', as reflected in 'before and after' scores on the CRIME-PICS II questionnaire. All three sets of results are compared by site and where appropriate by prisoner category.

Next, although it is recognised that they are not robust enough to be used as outcome measures, some data are presented (a) on the accommodation and employment status of some of the FOR participants, comparing their situation before and after imprisonment, and (b) on their self-reported levels of substance misuse and re-offending.

Finally, as mentioned above, we summarise the results of the one-year reconviction study of prisoners who took part in the Phase 1 Pathfinders.

Continuity of service

Levels of continuity of service are assessed here only in relation to Automatic Unconditional Release (AUR) prisoners (those serving under 12 months) since, unlike Automatic Conditional Release (ACR) prisoners, they are not subject to statutory supervision on release and are not therefore obliged to remain in contact. Receiving continuity of service is defined – as in the Phase 1 Pathfinder study (Lewis et al, 2003a) – as having some face-to-face contact with FOR staff (or their community links) beyond the day of release: this contact may be initiated either by the offender or by a team member.

Altogether, 198 AUR prisoners started the FOR programme and 153 completed it. At the time that we received the relevant records from the projects, 138 of the latter had been released. We have already seen (Chapter 4) that 28% of these 138 had *some* post-release contact with FOR staff or links. As Table 5.1 shows, a somewhat smaller proportion (22%) experienced face-to-face contact beyond the first day, our interim outcome measure. It is also clear, as already discussed, that the Hull team made contact with a much higher proportion of ex-prisoners than the other two projects. When measured by the tighter criterion of continuity of service, this gap is even wider: Hull achieved a continuity rate of 41%, compared with 10% in Lewes and only 6% in Parc (a striking contrast to Parc's good performance in this respect in Phase 1). The difference was statistically significant after controlling for individual factors such as age and OASys score (see Appendix A, Table A6).

This striking difference in continuity of service 'through the gate' therefore seems less dependent upon the individual characteristics of offenders than upon factors related to the individual areas or resettlement projects. The most obvious difference between the post-release arrangements at the three sites was that in Hull, the FOR facilitators based in the prison retained responsibility for contact with the prisoners after their release; while at Parc, this responsibility was fully handed over to a designated probation officer based in the community who had little, if any, pre-release contact with participants; and in Lewes, there was an arrangement somewhere between the two, whereby the prison facilitators shared the tasks with Crime Reduction Initiative (CRI) 'community links'. The above findings – and especially the major difference between Hull and Parc in terms of continuity – are consistent with the conclusion from a number of previous research studies that voluntary contact after release is affected above all by the extent to which offenders personally get to know their potential post-release contacts before they leave custody (see Maguire et al, 1997, 2000; Lewis et al, 2003a, p 48).

Table 5.1: AUR prisoners experiencing continuity of service, by prison

Prison	Number of released AUR prisoners who had started FOR	Number of released AUR prisoners who had completed FOR	AUR cases with continuity of service[a]		
			Number	% of 'starters'	% of 'completers'
Parc	51	47	3	6	6
Hull	72	51	21	29	41
Lewes	58	40	6	10	15
All sites	181	138	30	17	22

Note:
[a] Defined as face-to-face contact beyond the day of release.

Changes in CRIME-PICS scores

The second and third interim measures used in this study are based upon the CRIME-PICS II questionnaire and relate to changes in participants' pro-criminal attitudes and levels of perceived life problems. This instrument was selected because it has been found in previous studies to be related to reconviction (Raynor, 1998) and is hence useful as an early 'proxy' measure for reconviction rates (analysis of the current dataset also found a significant association with reconviction – see Appendix C). It has also been widely used in probation-based evaluation research, forming part of the standard battery of assessments for probation programmes. The instrument has five sub-scales. This section concentrates on two scales, which are based on the largest number of items and are therefore most sensitive to change: the G scale ('general attitudes to crime') and the P scale ('perception of current life problems').

CRIME-PICS II was intended to be administered at three stages:

- Stage 1: before commencing the programme.
- Stage 2: after completing session 12 of the programme and while still in prison.
- Stage 3: after completing the post-release phase of the programme.

Of the overall total of 278 offenders who completed the FOR programme 241 (87%) were assessed with CRIME-PICS II both at stage one and stage two.[1] A smaller number (92) completed a third CRIME-PICS following their release.

Table 5.2 shows that the level of change between the first and second CRIME-PICS scores was highly significant across all scales, and the level of change between second and third CRIME-PICS scores was significant for the G (general attitudes to crime) and P (perception of current life problems) scales. This indicates that the greatest changes occurred during the prison sentence (that is, between the first and second CRIME-PICS), but that improvements appeared to be maintained and some even increased after release.

Table 5.3 shows that the level of change in average CRIME-PICS scores varied significantly by both prisoner type and site. Lewes, for example, achieved the highest rate of attitude change for AUR prisoners (–7.1 compared with –6.0 in Hull and –5.9 in Parc). To ascertain whether levels of attitude change were statistically significant, paired sample t-tests were carried out for AUR participants. It emerged that highly significant levels of positive attitude change ($p < 0.01$) were achieved with such prisoners in all three sites. However, while reductions were also seen in all three sites in their levels of perceived life problems, the degree of change only reached statistical significance in Hull and Lewes.

---

[1] Non-completers did not fill in a second CRIME-PICS, and therefore no comparison can be made between them and completers in terms of attitude change.

Table 5.2: Changes in average CRIME-PICS II scores: all sites[a]

Scale	1st score (CP1)	2nd score (CP2)	3rd score (CP3)	Significance of change CP1 to CP2	CP2 to CP3
General attitudes to crime (G)	45.9	40.5	38.2	*	**
Anticipation of re-offending (A)	15.6	13.8	13.2	*	n/s
Victim hurt denial (V)	7.0	6.4	5.9	**	n/s
Evaluation of crime as worthwhile (E)	11.9	10.4	10.7	*	n/s
Perception of life problems (P)	32.1	29.0	25.1	*	*

Notes:
[a] CRIME-PICS (CP) 1 and 2, $n = 241$; CP3, $n = 92$.
* denotes significance at the 1% level.
** denotes significance at the 5% level.
n/s = not significant.

Turning to ACR prisoners, while the degree of attitude change tended to be less than for AUR prisoners, statistically significant attitude change was achieved across all three sites. Conversely, significant change in perceived life problems among this group of prisoners was found in Parc and Lewes only, where greater change was achieved among ACR prisoners compared with those on shorter sentences. (For previous research on the needs of, and resettlement work with, ACR prisoners, see Maguire and Raynor, 1997.)

Findings relating to change among young offenders (YOs) show that the degree of change overall was markedly less than among AUR and ACR participants. No statistically significant changes in levels of perceived life problems were found among YOs in either of the relevant sites, and a statistically significant change in attitudes was found only in Parc. However, these results should be treated with caution due to the small numbers of this type of prisoner in the samples.

Other changes, pre- to post-imprisonment

A final set of possible indicators of the impact of the Phase 2 Resettlement Pathfinders – admittedly less robust than those discussed above – can be derived from information about changes in various aspects of offenders' circumstances and behaviour after release, in comparison with their situation prior to imprisonment. These will be discussed under three main headings: accommodation and employment; substance misuse; and levels of self-reported re-offending.

Table 5.3: Change in average CRIME-PICS scores, by site and type of prison sentence[a]

HMP Parc	Average attitude score (G)		Average problem score (P)		Change in average scores	
Sentence type	Stage 1	Stage 2	Stage 1	Stage 2	Attitude change (+/−)	Problem change (+/−)
AUR (n = 43)	42.0	36.1	31.2	29.9	−5.9*	−1.3 n/s
ACR (n = 44)	43.4	39.0	31.3	27.9	−4.4*	−3.4*
YO (n = 19)	46.2	41.7	31.5	31.6	−4.5**	+0.1 n/s
HMP Hull	Average attitude score (G)		Average problem score (P)		Change in average scores	
Sentence type	Stage 1	Stage 2	Stage 1	Stage 2	Attitude change (+/−)	Problem change (+/−)
AUR (n = 52)	49.0	43.0	33.1	29.3	−6.0*	−3.8*
ACR (n = 23)	45.4	40.6	27.2	25.7	−4.8**	−1.5 n/s
YO (n = 9)	43.3	39.8	25.8	24.4	−3.5 n/s	−1.4 n/s
HMP Lewes	Average attitude score (G)		Average problem score (P)		Change in average scores	
Sentence type	Stage 1	Stage 2	Stage 1	Stage 2	Attitude change (+/−)	Problem change (+/−)
AUR (n = 35)	49.5	42.4	35.4	29.9	−7.1*	−5.5*
ACR (n = 16)	48.2	43.1	38.6	31.4	−5.1**	−7.2*

Notes:
* denotes significance at the 1% level.
** denotes significance at the 5% level.
n/s = not significant.
[a] Only CRIME-PICS 1 and 2 are included in the analysis as the number of CRIME-PICS 3 are deemed too small for reliable analysis once broken down by prison and sentence type.

Accommodation and employment

It is clear from previous literature (see, for example, Maguire et al, 1997; NACRO, 2000) that short-term prison sentences often worsen the situation of offenders in terms of their access to accommodation and employment. For example, rented property may be lost due to failure to keep up payments, while jobs may be lost due to the stigma of conviction or the hiatus in attendance. Hence, if the Pathfinder teams were able to assist offenders in preventing or replacing such losses – even if only to the extent that their accommodation and employment situations were no worse after leaving prison than they had been at the time of their arrest – this could be seen as an indicator of effective resettlement work.

We are able to compare the pre- and post-imprisonment accommodation and employment status of FOR participants who maintained any contact with the projects (and thus on whom post-release records were kept). We can also compare their *actual* status post-release with their *expected* status at the time they were first assessed in custody. These offenders, it is emphasised, are likely to have been more motivated to avoid re-offending, and in a more stable situation in terms of jobs and housing, than those who failed to stay in contact, so the results cannot be taken as applying to FOR participants as a whole.[2]

The above data were available from the CMRs of 97 offenders who had some contact (in person or by telephone or letter) after release. The post-release data related to different lengths of time after release for different offenders, depending on their last contact with project staff, but most described the situation at between one and three months after release. Table 5.4 shows that the proportion of these with 'permanent' accommodation (43%) was lower after release than it had been prior to their imprisonment (51%). However, the reduction was accounted for almost entirely by prisoners from Hull (which anyway started from a high baseline); in the other two sites, the proportions had changed little. The table also shows that, overall, ex-prisoners' actual housing situation turned out to be slightly better than they had expected during their sentence (only in Hull did expectations turn out to have been over-optimistic).

---

[2] It should also be noted that there were some discrepancies between the information about accommodation and employment status on the case management records (CMRs) and the answers given on this subject by the 71 offenders we interviewed after release. This may be attributable to the fact that interviews were conducted and CMRs completed at different points in time, and participants' status could have changed within a relatively short period of time.

Table 5.4: Comparison of pre-prison accommodation status with expectations on entering custody and actual status post-release (%)

	Permanent			Temporary		No fixed abode		In custody
Site	Pre	Expected	Post	Pre	Post	Pre	Post	Post
Parc	40	28	43	48	45	13	3	10
Hull	68	59	49	20	39	12	7	5
Lewes	31	31	31	25	56	44	6	6
All sites	51	41	43	32	44	18	5	7

Notes:
n = 97 offenders who were in contact after release, and on whom both pre- and post-release records were available. 'Expected' refers to expected accommodation status at time of assessment early in prison sentence.

Perhaps most encouraging, while 18% had been homeless before going into prison, only 5% were homeless after release. This change was accompanied by a corresponding rise in the numbers in temporary accommodation. However, it should be remembered that the above 97 offenders were not a random sample of all FOR participants, and it is likely that higher proportions remained homeless among those on whom there was no information.

A similar examination of employment status (see Table 5.5) reveals that there was a substantial decrease in levels of unemployment across all three sites, with an overall drop from 72% pre-imprisonment to 44% post-release. The proportion of individuals in employment rose from 25% to 34%, while the percentage enrolled in training or education rose from nil to 7%. Again, a comparison of expected levels of employment at the time of assessment in prison, with actual levels measured post-release, reveals that offenders were more than twice as likely to end up in employment as they had anticipated (at that point, only 17% had expected to find employment).

Table 5.5: Comparison of pre-prison employment status with expectations on entering custody and actual status post-release (%)

	Employed			Training		Unemployed		Inactive		In custody
Site	Pre	Expected	Post	Pre	Post	Pre	Post	Pre	Post	Post
Parc	33	33	43	0	5	65	38	3	5	10
Hull	15	2	24	0	7	81	51	5	12	5
Lewes	31	13	38	0	13	69	44	0	0	6
All sites	25	17	34	0	7	72	44	3	7	7

Notes:
n = 97 offenders who were in contact after release, and on whom both pre- and post-release records were available. 'Expected' refers to expected employment status at time of assessment early in prison sentence.

Taken together, the above findings suggest that offenders who complete FOR and who maintain contact post-release, are more likely to be employed after imprisonment than they were before it, and hence to confound the low expectations that most have at the beginning of their sentence. Their accommodation situation seems less likely to improve, but may be better protected than among short-term prisoners as a whole (compare NACRO, 2000). On the other hand, we have no information on FOR participants who did not maintain contact.

Substance misuse

Among the 71 individuals interviewed after release, 51 (72%) reported that they had had some form of substance misuse problem prior to taking the FOR programme. All 51 also admitted that they still had some problem with drugs or alcohol after release. However, as many as 80% of them claimed that the FOR programme had had some positive effect upon their drug/alcohol use. The main claims made were that they had reduced their overall intake, changed their main 'drug of choice' and/or were more likely to limit their use to Class C drugs. As Table 5.6 shows, there appeared to be a substantial shift away from heroin and cocaine towards cannabis. Findings of this kind based on interviews with offenders must of course be treated with caution, but the frequency with which positive claims and comments were made was striking. Examples of positive comments included:

'The programme is all about thinking and believing you can achieve things. I am a different person now and lead a different life. It was a combination of being ready to change and the programme gave me the final shove I needed to do that.'

'I have now learnt that to achieve and reach my goals I cannot do drugs so I keep occupied and healthy by going to the gym.'

Table 5.6: Self-reported main 'drug of choice' pre- and post-programme

Substance	Pre-FOR (%)	After release (%)
Heroin/cocaine	77	33
Ecstasy/amphetamine	8	7
Cannabis	4	51
Alcohol	12	9
Total ($n = 51$)[a]	101	100

Notes:
[a] Analysis is limited to 51 FOR participants interviewed after release, who stated that they had had a substance misuse problem prior to taking the programme.
Percentages do not always total 100 due to rounding.

Level of self-reported re-offending

FOR participants interviewed in the community were asked whether they had become involved in any criminal activities since their release from prison. Twenty-one (30%) of the 71 admitted to becoming involved in crime since being released, although only eight of these 21 individuals had subsequently been convicted of an offence. When those who had committed crimes were asked if there was anything more the programme could have done to help prevent them from doing so only three participants felt that more could have been done. One felt that he could have avoided re-offending if he had received more one-to-one attention while in prison. Another suggested having a mentor for post-release support who is independent from the probation service while the third felt he needed more help getting into drug rehabilitation prior to release.

Individuals who reported that they had not re-offended were asked whether the FOR programme had had any impact upon their decision to remain crime-free following their release from prison. Among the 50 individuals who reported that they had not re-offended, 41 (82%) claimed that the programme had helped them to avoid committing further crime. One commented for example that:

> 'FOR has made me look at things differently, I now realise crime doesn't pay, I
> just don't want to do it. It doesn't matter how desperate I am, I'd rather ring up
> probation for food vouchers than shoplift as I now look at consequences because of
> FOR.'

Phase 1 Pathfinders: one-year reconviction rates

As noted earlier, additional evidence of the effectiveness of the Resettlement Pathfinders, including that of the FOR programme, can be obtained from the one-year reconviction study we carried out on participants in the Phase 1 projects. As offenders were not allocated randomly to the projects, but joined on a voluntary basis, one cannot have full confidence in the results. Although we constructed a comparison group of short-term offenders who did not take part, and although these were similar to the participants in terms of static risk factors (for example, age and previous convictions), it was not possible to compare the two groups in terms of dynamic factors (such as substance abuse, or initial levels of motivation). Dynamic factors (which may be associated with a lower risk of reconviction) may have played a part in offenders' decisions to join the projects, so it cannot be assumed that the two groups were strictly comparable. On the other hand, some dynamic risk factors could be taken into account in comparisons between specific intervention groups (for example, those in individual prisons or those taking or not taking FOR), as we had OASys scores for most participants. Finally, it is emphasised that a one-year reconviction study is usually considered less reliable than a two-year study (Colledge et al, 1999), and that the numbers of offenders completing the FOR programme were relatively small. Nevertheless, with these provisos, the results are worth publishing, as they provide some indicative evidence about effectiveness, especially in relation to differences between projects (which adopted a variety of approaches to resettlement) and to post-release contact.

Phase 1 of the Resettlement Pathfinders involved seven projects, four of which did not continue into Phase 2. These were based in six prisons holding males and one holding females (the neighbouring establishments of Springhill and Woodhill were covered by the same project, and are counted here as one prison). In three projects the lead was taken by voluntary organisations, and in four by probation services:

- Voluntary led:
  - o Birmingham
  - o Lewes
  - o Wandsworth
- Probation led:
  - o Hull
  - o Parc
  - o Springhill/Woodhill
  - o Durham Low Newton (female).

Altogether, 1,081 prisoners – all serving under 12 months – joined the Pathfinders, and 921 of these were still 'members' at the point of release. Of these, 397 had some contact post-release with project staff or designated community links. In the three probation-led projects in male prisons, some participants took part in the FOR programme: this was started by 141 and completed by 114 prisoners. Two of the voluntary-led projects, Lewes and Wandsworth, used trained volunteer mentors for post-release contact with offenders.

Methodology

The researchers obtained one-year reconviction data from the Home Office Offenders Index (OI) for the Pathfinder participants and comparison groups. The OI also generated 'Offender Group Reconviction Scale' (OGRS2) scores for each offender at the point of leaving prison, allowing the calculation of predicted rates of reconviction for both groups. OGRS2 has been calculated to give predicted reconviction rates at the two-year point. When comparing predicted and actual rates, we therefore converted each male offender's OGRS2 score into a 'one-year equivalent', based on previous research (see Appendix C). However, this was not feasible for female offenders.

A simple comparison between participants' predicted and actual reconviction rates could be distorted by a number of factors, including local differences and changes over time in conviction patterns. It is therefore important also to examine the predicted and actual recorded reconvictions of similar (ideally local) groups of offenders who have not undergone the intervention in question. We drew comparison groups of offenders from each of the prisons that hosted the Phase I Resettlement Pathfinder projects, using randomly selected samples of offenders who were in the prisons in 1999, the year before the projects were established. However, Durham Low Newton was in the process of becoming an all-women's prison in 1999 and could not provide a sufficient comparison group of female offenders for that period. A comparison group was therefore drawn from two other women's prisons (Askham Grange and Styal) in the north of England.

The offenders whose details were run through the OI comprised the 1,081 participants from the seven original Pathfinders and 2,450 short-term prisoners to be used as comparisons. As is normal with studies of this kind (see, for example, Friendship et al, 2001; Francis et al, 2002), a fair proportion of offenders in both groups could not be identified on the OI. After a careful verification process, 199 (18%) of the 1,081 participants and 604 (25%) of the 2,450 comparisons were excluded as non-matches and doubtful matches. This left us with two main sets of offenders to analyse and compare in terms of reconvictions:

- the *intervention groups* of 764 males and 118 females who had joined the Phase I Pathfinders; and
- the *comparison groups* of 1,542 males and 304 females who had been in the same (or, in the case of females, similar) prisons in the year before the projects began.

The intervention groups had considerably higher mean OGRS2 scores (that is, a generally higher risk of reconviction) than the comparison groups, suggesting that project staff had generally targeted their recruitment efforts more strongly at those prisoners with greater (criminogenic) problems and needs, and/or that the latter had been more attracted to the projects than those with low needs. In addition, there was considerable variation between the different prisons: for example, Hull Pathfinder participants had an average two-year predicted reconviction rate of 73%, compared with 58% in Springhill and Woodhill combined. These variations make it necessary to control throughout the analysis for differences in OGRS2 scores.

Finally, female prisoners had generally higher risk scores than males, but it should be noted that the OGRS2 instrument is less reliable for females than males. The analysis was therefore conducted separately for female and male offenders.

Table 5.7: Predicted two-year and one-year reconviction rates, and actual one-year reconviction rates: Phase I intervention groups and comparison groups, by sex (%)

	Intervention groups				Comparison groups			
	Reconviction rate				Reconviction rate			
	Predicted		Actual	Actual	Predicted		Actual	Actual
	2 years	I year	I year	I year minus predicted I year	2 years	I year	I year	I year minus pre-dicted I year
Male prisoners	65	51	55	+4	57	43	45	+2
Female prisoners[a]	69	–	75	–	58	–	60	–

Notes:
Male prisoners intervention groups $n = 764$, comparison groups $n = 1,542$. Female intervention groups $n = 118$, comparison groups $n = 304$.
Predicted one-year reconviction rates were derived from the 'conversion table' in Appendix C. This was not possible for female offenders.
[a] As OGRS2 is less reliable for females than males, the figures in this row should be regarded with caution.

Results

Table 5.7 shows the overall reconviction rates after 12 months for the intervention groups (including non-completers) and comparison groups, divided by sex of the offenders. It also shows the reconviction rates which were predicted through OGRS2 (a) after two years (the standard OGRS2 prediction period) and (b) after 12 months (as recalculated using the table shown in Appendix C).

Where male offenders are concerned, both the intervention and the comparison groups appear to have done slightly 'worse' than predicted by OGRS2 (or, more accurately, by our conversion of the two-year predicted rate into a one-year rate). However, the differences were not statistically significant. Among female offenders, both the intervention and the comparison groups appear to have done much worse than expected, having already passed their two-year predicted reconviction rates after just 12 months. However, as OGRS2 is less reliable for females than for males, not too much should be read into this result.

These 'headline figures' indicate that the Pathfinders had no immediately obvious impact on reconviction rates 'across the board'. However, it is also important to look for possible differential effects on particular subgroups of participants. These were explored through both bi-variate and multi-variate analysis.

Bi-variate analysis

First of all, a distinction can be made between those offenders who remained 'members' of the Pathfinders throughout their time in custody, and those who joined the projects but 'dropped out' before their release. Altogether, 160 of the original 1,081 participants dropped out (see Lewis et al, 2003a). Most of these did so involuntarily, as they were unexpectedly transferred or released on Home Detention Curfew. Most, too, left before any work could be done with them in prison. An analysis of reconviction rates for male 'completers' and 'drop-outs' found that the completers did better than drop-outs in relation to their predicted rates (especially in the higher risk bands), but again the differences were not statistically significant. Moreover, the 'completers' as a whole did no better than the comparison groups.

Some differences between prisons were apparent, broadly echoing differences in degree of attitude change found in the Phase 1 evaluation (Lewis et al, 2003a, 2003b).[3] Probation-led projects as a group had better reconviction outcomes than those led by voluntary agencies, although the difference did not reach statistical significance at the 5% level. The best outcomes by some distance (in relation to both their predicted outcomes and their control groups) were achieved by Parc and Springhill/Woodhill – both probation-led schemes – and the worst by Birmingham (which was voluntary-led).

However, the only statistically significant differences in reconviction outcomes found in bi-variate analysis related to *post-release contact* (or 'continuity'). As Table 5.8 shows, male prisoners who had contact with Pathfinder staff or community links after release were reconvicted below their predicted rate, while those who had no contact were reconvicted at a rate six percentage points above that predicted.[4] This appears to be an important finding, which supports the widely held view – reflected in the establishment of the National Offender Management Service and the development of regional resettlement schemes – that continuity of service 'through the gate' is of major importance to the effectiveness of any resettlement programme. (It also, incidentally, supports our choice in the initial study of 'continuity' as a proxy measure of effectiveness.)

A further, surprising aspect of this analysis was that post-release contact with *volunteer mentors* was associated with the greatest reduction in predicted reconviction rates. Although participants' reconviction outcomes were relatively poor overall in the two prisons (Lewes and Wandsworth) that used mentors,

---

[3] More generally, individuals' scores on the CRIME-PICS 'G' scale were strongly associated with actual reconviction rates, as were OASys scores (see Appendix D).

[4] This difference was statistically significant at the 5% level. See Appendix A, Figure A1 for a visual representation of the difference in each prison.

Table 5.8: Predicted and actual one-year reconviction rates of males in intervention groups who had and did not have post-release contact, and male comparison groups (%)

Post-release contact [a]	Intervention groups			Comparison groups		
	One-year reconviction rate			One-year reconviction rate		
	Predicted	Actual	Actual minus pre-dicted	Predicted	Actual	Actual minus pre-dicted
Yes	49	48	−1	–	–	–
No	53	59	+6	43	45	+2

Notes:
Intervention groups, post-release contact *n* = 291.
Intervention groups, no post-release contact *n* = 473.
Comparison groups *n* = 1,542.
[a] Significant in t-test, post-release contact *p* = 0.026.

the situation was reversed for the 55 prisoners who kept contact with a mentor. Indeed, this was one of the only cases in which a subsection of the intervention group significantly 'outperformed' the comparison group. The numbers involved were small, so the results must be treated with caution, but the differences were statistically significant (see Appendix A, Table A7). It appears, then, that if these projects helped to bring about any major changes among participants, this took place *post-release* (that is, through contact with the mentors) rather than in prison. This is further supported by the finding that virtually no changes were apparent among the 55 prisoners in question between CRIME-PICS II scores obtained early and late in their prison sentences. This is consistent with the fact that these projects did not run FOR (attendance at which was associated with significant changes in attitude scores). The finding also raises interesting questions about the relative importance of pre- and post-release work, and of professional and volunteer input, in the reduction of reconviction.

Although reconviction results were generally best in the probation-led projects in the male prisons – all of which ran the FOR programme – there was no evidence that taking FOR per se had any impact on reconviction rates, either in relation to other Pathfinder participants, or to comparison groups. Indeed, within these projects, offenders who completed the programme did no better (relative to predicted risk) than others who did not take it or dropped out. Nevertheless, there is some evidence that, while attendance at FOR on its own may have had no impact on reconviction rates, FOR *followed up by post-release work* may have had an impact. Of 47 offenders who completed FOR but did no work subsequently with Pathfinder staff or links, 36 (77%) were reconvicted. By contrast, of 38 who completed FOR and then went on to work with staff post-release, only 14 (37%) were reconvicted. While the latter group had a lower risk profile than the former, the difference was still statistically significant after controlling for OGRS2 scores. This finding should be considered in conjunction with the Phase I finding (Lewis et al, 2003a, 2003b) that prisoners who took FOR were significantly more likely than others to maintain contact after release: in other words, while taking the programme per se did not produce lower reconviction rates, it was associated with increased continuity, which in turn was associated with lower reconviction rates.

Multi-variate analysis

In order to determine whether the variables that appeared from bi-variate analysis to affect reconviction rates remained independently significant when other factors were controlled for, the data were also subjected to multi-variate analysis. As the dependent variable (reconviction) was binary in character, the appropriate procedure was logistic regression.

Table 5.9 shows the results of a logistic regression seeking to explain the differing one-year reconviction rates of offenders who participated in the six Pathfinders in male prisons. OGRS2 scores – converted, as described earlier, into a one-year equivalent – were included to control for (static) risk of reconviction. The regression was also run (on lower numbers of offenders) with the inclusion of OASys and CRIME-PICS II scores, in order to control for dynamic risk factors, but this was found to make no difference to the results in terms of which variables emerged as independently statistically significant.

Table 5.9: Regression model predicting higher one-year reconviction rate

Variable	Exp (B)	Sig.
OGRS2 (converted to one year)	129.863	*
Springhill/Woodhill	0.359	*
Parc	0.263	*
Post-release contact (mentor)	0.355	*
Post-release contact (other)	0.771	–
Completed FOR	1.752	–

Notes:
An odds ratio (Exp (B)) below 1.0 means that the chances are less than even that the reconviction rate will be higher: thus, for example, post-release contact was less likely to produce a higher reconviction rate than no post-release contact.
$n = 764$ male participants in Phase I Pathfinders.
* denotes significance at the 1% level.

The results confirm – and add a slightly different perspective to – the general indications from the bi-variate analysis. The only independent variables (apart from OGRS2) that emerged as statistically significantly associated with reconviction rates were membership of particular projects, and post-release contact with a mentor. In short, when other factors were controlled for, participants from Springhill/Woodhill or Parc, and prisoners seen post-release by mentors attached to the Lewes or Wandsworth projects, tended to do better than others. Despite the fact that the two prisons with the most encouraging results were probation-led, further regression analysis found no significant difference in reconviction rates between probation- and voluntary-led projects as a whole: the broad picture to emerge was that, while prisoners in voluntary-led projects did relatively poorly if they had no later contact in the community, those who saw mentors after release did exceptionally well.

Again, completing the FOR programme did not emerge as a significant factor in reducing reconviction. However, further regression analysis (in this case controlling for dynamic as well as static risk factors, as OASys scores were available for all but one FOR completers) confirmed the earlier finding from bi-variate analysis that, among offenders who completed FOR, those who engaged in some kind of work with Pathfinder staff after their release were significantly less likely to be reconvicted than those who finished the programme but left without further contact (see Table 5.10). It is also worth noting that whether or not contact was established emerged as much more important than how long any contact lasted.

Outcomes: summary and discussion

We end this chapter with a brief summary and discussion of the main findings from both phases of the Resettlement Pathfinders, drawing out some of their possible implications.

Table 5.10: Regression model predicting higher one-year reconviction rate: only those prisoners who completed the FOR programme

Variable	Exp (B)	Sig.
OGRS2 (converted to one year)	16.980	*
OASys score	1.029	*
Post-release work	0.230	*
Prison in which located	–	–

Notes:
* denotes significance at the 5% level.
n = 85 male participants in Phase 1 Pathfinders who completed FOR.

The Phase 2 results

Overall, our chosen interim indicators of effectiveness tell an encouraging story in relation to the three Pathfinders evaluated under Phase 2. All three sites showed more significant positive changes in both crime-prone attitudes and self-reported problems than in the first phase of the Resettlement Pathfinders (Lewis et al, 2003a), although these varied somewhat according to the type and age of the prisoner. This suggests that a more systematic focus on project implementation and on delivering the FOR programme to more participants has improved the impact on prisoners' thinking skills and their abilities to problem solve in all the three project sites.

Second, levels of post-release contact with AUR prisoners, as in the first phase of the Pathfinders, comfortably exceeded those found in a previous study of voluntary aftercare as undertaken by the probation service alone (Maguire et al, 1997, 2000). On the other hand, as a group the three projects did not achieve the overall levels found in the first Pathfinders. In the current study, 17% of all prisoners who started the programme received continuity of service 'through the gate': this compares with 29% across all seven Pathfinders involved in the first phase. There were, however, major differences in performance between the sites. Lewes' level of continuity slipped from 22% in the first phase to 10% in this second phase, and Parc saw a particularly steep drop, from 33% (when post-release work was largely undertaken ad hoc by project staff) to just 6% (when it was transferred to outside probation officers).[5] The exception was Hull, where the level of continuity fell only slightly, from 32% to 29%.

It appears likely from both the previous and the current study that levels of continuity are strongly affected by the way the post-release service is organised. As discussed earlier, Hull's approach of using the same facilitators for both pre-release and post-release work led in both phases to relatively high levels of continuity of service 'through the gate'. On the other hand, Parc's approach in Phase 2 of commissioning outside probation officers to take on AUR prisoners in addition to their statutory (ACR and DCR) caseloads does not appear to have been successful in terms of contact levels. It is likely that part of the explanation for this is that offenders are more likely to keep appointments to see people if they have already got to know them in prison. General antipathy to probation officers (unless they are well known to the offender) may also play a part. However, it also has to be remembered that the distances between ex-prisoners' homes and the offices where they were to be seen post-release, were for the most part considerably shorter in Hull than in South Wales (and to a lesser extent in the Brighton area).

---

[5] It should be noted that Parc's high continuity rate in the first phase was helped by its recruitment of a relatively small number of prisoners: as a late addition to the Pathfinders, it took on only 49 participants, compared with an average of around 170 in the other six schemes (Lewis et al, 2003a, p 30).

Comparisons were made of offenders' accommodation and employment status prior to entering prison, their expectations at the time of assessment early in their sentence and their actual status one to three months after release. These data could be collected only on those who had remained in contact with the project staff after release, so the results are likely to be better than would have been the case for all FOR participants and must therefore be treated with caution. With this proviso, the results are positive in terms of employment, where as many as 41% were found to be employed or in training post-release, compared with only 25% of the same group of offenders before release. Moreover, the actual employment situation turned out to be much better than expected: when assessed early in their sentence, only 17% had expected to get a job.

The results regarding accommodation were less encouraging, especially in Hull, where the proportion in 'permanent' accommodation fell from 68% pre-imprisonment to 49% post-release. On the other hand, the proportion of offenders with 'no fixed abode' among the 97 for whom accommodation information was available fell markedly at all three sites, and overall from 18% to just 5% (it should, however, be remembered that a higher percentage of offenders not in contact post-release are likely to have been of no fixed abode).

Finally, among the 51 offenders interviewed post-release who reported that they had had a substance misuse problem before going to prison, 80% claimed that the programme had helped them to control it to some extent after release – principally by adopting a less harmful 'drug of choice'. Similarly, of the 70% of interviewees who claimed that they had not offended since release, 82% considered that the programme had helped them to achieve this. These results may, however, reflect a degree of over-optimism among these interviewees (who were as a group likely to have been more receptive to the programme than FOR participants as a whole).

Conclusions from the Phase 1 reconviction analysis

It is re-emphasised that the results from the reconviction analysis of participants from Phase 1 of the Resettlement Pathfinders must be treated with caution, as they may be subject to selection effects (participation being voluntary) and are based on one-year follow-up only. Nevertheless, they are largely in tune with findings from both phases concerning changes in attitudes and problems (as measured by CRIME-PICS II and OASys), and provide further indicative evidence as to which aspects of resettlement work may be critical to its effectiveness. The main (tentative) conclusions that emerge are:

(a) The Phase 1 Pathfinders had no immediately obvious impact on reconviction rates 'across the board'. Male participants were not reconvicted at a significantly different rate than predicted by OGRS2, nor (after controlling for risk) than that of prisoners in the comparison groups. Moreover, female participants were reconvicted at *higher* than expected rates, although it should be borne in mind that the prediction instrument is less reliable for females.

(b) There were, however, some significant differences in reconviction rates (again after controlling for risk) between particular groups of participants. At first sight, some of these may seem contradictory. On the one hand, offenders from two probation-led projects did significantly better than those in other projects; on the other, prisoners from the two voluntary-led projects who had post-release contact with mentors also had exceptionally low reconviction rates.

(c) There was no evidence that taking the FOR programme per se affected reconviction rates. However, among prisoners who completed FOR, those who engaged in post-release work did significantly better than those who did not.

As will be discussed in the concluding chapter (Chapter 7), a possible implication of these findings – taken in conjunction with the Phase 2 impact data discussed above – is that successful resettlement depends *both* upon systematic attention to thinking skills and motivation in prison (as practised by the probation-led projects) *and* post-release contact with someone with whom the offender has developed a sympathetic relationship while in prison.

Organisational and implementation issues

This penultimate chapter presents findings and raises issues arising from the organisational structures and arrangements surrounding the implementation of the Phase 2 Resettlement Pathfinders and the delivery of the FOR programme. It begins with a look at organisational issues, then outlines the main stages of prisoners' progress, from recruitment and assessment to post-release follow-up. Throughout, particular attention will be paid to any obstacles to the effective delivery of the interventions.

Between 7 October 2002 and 31 July 2003, regular visits were made to each of the three sites to observe various FOR sessions. Interviews were undertaken with the treatment managers and tutors, designed to elicit information about staff training and supervision, recruitment and assessment procedures and interviewees' experiences of delivering the programme. The questionnaires covered the following areas:

- the nature of pre-release work carried out with the prisoners;
- the integration of the FOR programme within the prison, with particular reference to linkage with in-house services;
- the mechanisms for ensuring that the prisoners receive adequate post-release support following their release into the community.

In addition, systematic analysis was undertaken of all relevant documentation, including quarterly monitoring forms, case management records and OASys and CRIME-PICS II assessments.

Organisational issues

We begin by briefly presenting the main findings on each of the following organisational issues:

- management and staffing;
- staff training;
- facilities;
- relationships with prison management;
- relationships with prison staff;

- links with prison services;
- recruitment of offenders to the programme.

Management and staffing

A lack of permanent, dedicated FOR staff was a problem for both Lewes and Hull at various stages throughout the programme. While staffing problems were overcome to some extent in Lewes, problems remained in Hull.

At the beginning of Phase 2 of the Pathfinders, in July 2002, the project in HMP Lewes had only one full-time member of staff (the resettlement manager) and a pool of four part-time FOR tutors (consisting mainly of prison officers whose main responsibilities involved general prison duties). The mentors used in Phase 1 had left, leaving a gap in post-release arrangements. At this time, the resettlement manager was not only responsible for bridging the gap between the prison and the community and for post-release contact with participants in the Brighton area, but also had to oversee the delivery of the programme in the prison. By a year later, however, the staff group had grown to include:

- the resettlement manager;
- the part-time tutors (prison officers);
- a programme manager (appointed January 2003);
- a senior facilitator;
- one full-time tutor (prison officer);
- a seconded part-time tutor (probation officer);
- a part-time administrator (appointed October 2002);
- a part-time community link probation officer;
- two part-time community link workers (employed by Crime Reduction Initiative [CRI]).

The programme manager was primarily responsible for accessing the resources needed to run the programme within the prison and supervised the four prison officers who had been trained as FOR tutors. The community link officer was seconded to the programme on a part-time basis from Sussex probation service. His role included facilitating on the FOR programme and implementing post-release work with participants who were conditionally released in the Brighton area. Those returning to Worthing or Eastbourne were supervised by the locally based community workers.

With a full team finally in place, the resettlement manager reported that 'staff roles have become more defined within the team' and 'everyone is now in a position where they feel that they can actually get up and do what they're supposed to be doing, without questioning it'. The changes also meant that each of the programme tutors had the opportunity to facilitate a number of groups, which he believed had had a significant impact on the quality of programme delivery.

In HMP Hull, the Pathfinder staff-base comprised one senior prison officer and one probation officer who took on the role of treatment manager. Two full-time probation support officers (both trained in motivational interviewing and OASys) also worked on the programme, one of whom assumed the role of throughcare manager. Beyond this, the team had to rely on temporary and part-time staff. General support was provided by a part-time administrative officer. Two prison psychologists trained as tutors were temporarily seconded to the Pathfinder, but were withdrawn for other duties. Similarly, five Probation Service Officers (PSOs) and two R&R[1]-trained prison officers were also fully trained as tutors during the evaluation period, but soon returned to normal prison duties.

This uncertainty around staffing was frustrating for the project team and was felt by the managers to have negatively affected the project. One of the reasons for the temporary secondments was that earlier staff turnover had been high due to temporary tutors leaving the team to take up permanent posts. The problem was to some extent managed by seconding staff from other departments for short periods, but on occasion it was not possible to run groups due to a lack of trained tutors.

Towards the end of the evaluation period, Hull appointed a throughcare manager to increase the continuity between the pre- and post-release phases of the programme. This was said to have increased the trust and confidence of offenders and to have improved post-release attendance rates.

HMP Parc had the most stable staffing situation, the FOR team being based within the well-established Offending Behaviour Programmes Unit and able to draw on the unit's resources. However, although the managers had access to a pool of seven FOR-trained tutors, a general increase during the evaluation period in other programmes being run in the prison meant that they were not always available to facilitate on the FOR programme. Consequently, whereas previously up to four tutors were able to run a programme at any one time (that is, two programmes running concurrently), the pressure on tutors meant that by the second year of the project only one group could run at a time.

Staff training

Staff interviewed by the researchers generally felt that the programme training had been excellent and were satisfied that the 'booster' training sessions (for both FOR tutors and community links) hosted periodically by the programme's authors gave them adequate opportunity to update their skills. The recent addition of the FOR

---

[1] R&R (Reasoning and Rehabilitation) is a cognitive behavioural programme delivered both in prisons and in the community.

programme manual for the post-release phase was well received by the community links in all three sites.

Video recordings of treatment sessions were used by the treatment managers in Hull and Parc, as well as by the senior facilitator in Lewes, to provide feedback on programme delivery during in-house training sessions. In addition, staff in the three sites supported each other with informal feedback following sessions and had regular team meetings. The team at Lewes also benefited from external supervision, feedback and training from an expert specially employed by T3 for this purpose. The staff across all three sites felt that a combination of informal feedback and more objective feedback from a supervisory position was considered to be vital in order to maintain treatment integrity.

Facilities

Hull and Parc had regular access to designated programme facilities, including separate premises for classroom and administrative work. However, at Lewes, due to a lack of adequate treatment facilities, programme sessions were run in the prison chapel. While this was available to the FOR team every morning, it did not benefit from the furniture and equipment found in a typical classroom, including desks. Although this was not ideal, the tutors asserted that it did not have a major effect on the delivery of the programme.

Relationships with prison management

Strong and visible support from senior management within the prison was seen by staff as vital to the development and continuing success of the FOR programme. Such support was evident in Parc and Hull, and to a lesser extent in Lewes. In Hull, for example, the governor was familiar with the aims and objectives of FOR and endorsed the programme by attending quarterly team meetings, while a staff member at Parc commented:

> 'I cannot criticise the support and the resources they [senior management at Parc] have made available for FOR. They have made people available; they have a commitment to training, to setting up the OBPU [Offending Behaviour Programmes Unit]. They have given a high status to FOR and have not stood in the way of us developing this programme.'

The appointment of a programme manager in Lewes ensured that the FOR team had a prison officer dedicated to the programme at all times, and that a treatment room was always available. However, he did not attend team meetings and was only consulted if difficulties arose with the running of the programme.

Importantly, too, senior-level support in all three prisons meant that prisoners were removed from the programme only for disciplinary reasons or Home Detention Curfew, rather than through unexpected transfers to other prisons, which had been a problem for some schemes in the Phase 1 Pathfinders (Lewis et al, 2003a).

Relationships with prison staff

Working relationships between FOR and prison staff were reported by the project managers to have improved substantially in all three sites since the programme was first introduced.

Staff training sessions were run on a regular basis in both Parc and Hull, with the aim of increasing programme awareness among the prison officers. Several tutors commented on the positive impact these training sessions had on the wing officers in terms of increased cooperation, such as unlocking prisoners to send them to sessions on time, and expressed an appreciation of the work carried out by the FOR team. For example:

> 'We have a lockdown on the last Wednesday of every month, which is dedicated to training and since that has been happening things have been a lot better. Before some of the officers were quite hostile … but now they understand the work we do and have been a lot more positive about the programme.'

> 'It is improving. They used to be very dubious and looked upon us in the unit as a soft touch. It has taken a long time to get where we are now and a lot more staff are aware of what we are trying to do.'

In Lewes, there was no formal system in place to raise awareness of the programme among wing officers. Nonetheless, having a full-time prison officer allocated to the FOR team helped to establish better communication links between the FOR staff and wing officers. Being present on the wing and known to the wing officers, this officer was able to raise the awareness of prison staff to the aims and objectives of the FOR programme.

The programme at Hull had over time become increasingly well integrated into the wider prison regime. For example, on a number of occasions programme staff adopted the personal officers' duties, following discussions about FOR participants:

> 'Actually, I think, and this is just a personal opinion. When we take a group of prisoners on Pathfinders, we actually become their personal officers.… I think it is a compromise with the wings that we are in a position to do the things that a personal officer would normally do.'

Feedback between programme staff and personal officers also took place in Parc and Lewes, albeit to a lesser extent. In Lewes, it occurred routinely in cases where a prisoner was at risk of self-harm or had become particularly upset during a session. In Parc, if a prisoner was undergoing counselling, programme staff informed the counsellor that they had joined FOR.

Links with prison services

Access to in-house services was readily available, and programme staff in all three sites frequently took advantage of the support provided to meet the resettlement needs of FOR participants. In keeping with the programme's objective of boosting motivation, FOR staff tended to encourage prisoners to self-refer; in addition, unofficial fast-tracking systems tended to operate, whereby prisoners with specific or urgent needs could be referred to appropriate internal agencies at any point in the intervention. Similarly, several of the in-house service providers, notably CARATS (Counselling, Advice, Referral, Assessment and Throughcare Services) workers, counsellors and careers officers, directed prisoners meeting the FOR criteria on to the programme and demonstrated cooperation by attending the Marketplace sessions:

> 'We can fast-track people on our project with CARATS, you know they're quite busy, they got a five-week waiting list so if someone identifies with us that they would like some help with issues around drugs we can, I can go to CARATS and they can fast-track them, get them seen quicker.'

> 'We are vitally important to CARATS workers so we make a point of inviting both counsellors and CARATS workers to session 12. The thing about session 12 is that we not only have the external agencies but the internal workers as well, we have careers officers and drug workers from inside the prison so inside agencies can meet outside agencies. This prison is developing an intermeshing professional relationship between careers, housing, education, probation, CARATS workers and counselling.'

In addition, a 'one-stop-shop' was set up in Hull, which aimed to integrate services providing housing, benefits and employment within the prison. Although the service was in its infancy, it is thought by the project manager to have provided greater continuity and links with outside agencies for prisoners nearing release. An 'employment link worker' was also seconded on a permanent basis to Parc from Job Centre Plus. Similarly, a new Call Centre course, run by British Telecom, was set up in Parc. While it was hoped that this programme would work effectively alongside FOR, initial lack of communication meant that the two programmes were for a period competing for participants.

Recruitment of prisoners to the programme

Participation in the FOR programme was entirely voluntary, and each team had a strategy for recruiting suitable prisoners. The main objective was to ensure that, as far as possible, all those eligible were offered the chance to join. In Parc, for example, a variety of strategies were employed:

- Two FOR tutors were responsible for contributing on behalf of the team to the induction meetings attended by offenders entering the prison. Any deemed eligible were informed of the programme and given a flyer to take back to their cells. One of the tutors then returned to see the prisoner a couple of days later to ask him again whether he wished to join the programme.
- The roll-count sheet for the whole prison was regularly examined and each name checked for suitability. Tutors then approached all eligible prisoners identified.
- Prison officers, counsellors, seconded probation officers and other in-house service providers could refer on to the programme.
- Posters and leaflets were available on all wings, and any prisoner interested was able to self-refer by submitting a general application via a prison officer.

Similarly, in Hull:

- FOR staff identified eligible clients from the reception lists and then approached all appropriate prisoners.
- Self-referral was also encouraged and awareness raised with posters and leaflets available throughout the wings.

Finally, in Lewes, all eligible prisoners were identified from a database of new prisoners. They were then sent a leaflet asking them if they would like to participate on the programme. The prisoners were asked to return the application form via a prison officer, indicating whether they would like to attend the FOR or not. A FOR tutor also visited all the inmates a couple of days later to ask them if they wished to join the programme. If they agreed, they were usually given a brief overview of what to expect from the programme. In addition, posters and leaflets were available on the wings so that any prisoner interested in participating could self-refer by submitting a general application.

Issues in service delivery

The following sections present findings relating to the delivery of the packages of interventions offered by each of the Pathfinder projects. We begin with a brief description of the basic elements of such packages common to all the projects. This is followed by discussions of delivery issues relating to:

- assessment;
- action plans and prioritisation of problems;
- case management;
- attrition during custody;
- arrangements for post-release contact.

Common features of the delivery process

Once prisoners had agreed to join the Pathfinder and attend the FOR programme, they went through a number of stages of the delivery process. Although there was some variation between the sites in how these were organised, the basic sequence of delivery was the same in each:

- OASys and CRIME-PICS II assessments were carried out with each prisoner, ideally prior to session 1.
- An initial action plan was subsequently devised for each individual with the aim of addressing problems identified during the assessment. All of the work undertaken with prisoners pre-release was recorded on a case-related activity form attached to the case management record (CMR).
- A pre-session meeting was held a few days before the programme was due to start, enabling the prisoners to meet the tutors and other prisoners. These meetings provided an opportunity for tutors to establish ground rules, while the prisoners could ask questions, discuss any reservations they might have and confirm that they wished to continue with the programme.
- The 12-session programme was delivered over a four-week period. Midway through the programme, at session 7, prisoners had a one-to-one interview with a tutor to reassess their goals in preparation for session 12 – the Marketplace session. Session 12 was a crucial part of the throughcare process and provided prisoners with the opportunity to meet their community probation link, obtain advice and make appointments with a range of statutory and non-statutory community-based agencies.
- A revision to the programme was the inclusion of an additional one-to-one interview – session 13, Free to Change. This final session marked the end of Phase 1 of the programme and was usually delivered by the tutor some weeks after the programme finished, as close as practicable to the prisoner's release date. If, however, a prisoner was due for release immediately following session 12, the interview was carried out after release by the community link. The aim of this session was to provide prisoners with a final review of their motivation and skills and emphasise the support available to them in the community.
- In Parc and Lewes, the CMR was forwarded to the FOR probation link in the community, along with a copy of the prisoner's OASys. In Hull, the CMR was kept in prison as the programme staff fulfilled the role of community contact.
- All progress made post-release was then recorded on the CMR. In some cases a print out of the probation record from the CRAMS computerised record system was attached. This provided more detail on the outcome of the post-release phase.

Assessment

Staff in all three sites demonstrated clear understanding of the need for OASys and CRIME-PICS II assessments to be completed and initial action plans to be devised on the CMR for each prisoner prior to the start of each programme. According to one tutor, the OASys assessment tool is extremely relevant to the FOR programme as it 'gives you a thorough understanding of your group before you begin. You can really target and make the material very real for them by using examples that you know reflect people's problems'.

However, staff were unanimous in their opinion that, despite amendments to shorten and simplify the OASys assessment, it was too time-consuming and repetitive and needed further simplification. Several tutors who reported that they found the assessments challenging, and were subsequently spending too long completing the forms, identified a need for further training. Indeed, staff at all three sites mentioned instances of OASys assessments still being done midway through a programme. This was a particular problem in Lewes, where only one member of the team had experience in working with OASys.

Action plans: targeting and prioritisation of problems

Table 6.1 shows the types of problems highlighted in participants' individual action plans as having the highest priority for intervention. In each case, project staff recorded up to three key problems to be targeted. There were considerable differences between the sites. For example, Lewes saw accommodation as a key problem for almost two thirds of its participants, while Hull targeted accommodation in only 31% of cases. This may reflect both the differing natures of the housing markets in the two areas and the orientation of the staff (CRI was a voluntary agency with considerable experience in the housing field).

Other obvious differences include relatively low targeting of drugs problems in Parc, and of 'thinking skills' and 'lifestyle and associates' in Lewes. The latter finding was also evident in the first Pathfinders analysis, and is probably explained by the more 'practical' focus of the voluntary agency-led, as opposed to probation-led, resettlement project in Lewes.

Table 6.2 shows only those problems that were identified as the 'number one' priority on each CMR. Overall, drugs were clearly the highest priority for action (coming out top in a third of all cases). Accommodation, thinking skills and alcohol were the only other problems identified as the top priority in more than 5% of all cases.

Table 6.1: Key problems identified in action plans, by site (%)

Problem[a]	Parc	Lewes	Hull
Drugs	46	60	61
Accommodation[b]	35	65	31
Thinking skills[b]	58	22	47
Alcohol[b]	28	26	13
Lifestyle and associates[b]	32	22	46
Education/training	13	27	20
Attitudes[b]	15	7	27
Employment	36	35	44
Emotional well-being[b]	11	8	2
Financial management[b]	14	5	4
Relationships	12	17	5

Notes:
n = 281. Percentages do not total 100 as participants could give more than one response.
[a] Problems identified in top three key problems on the CMR.
[b] Chi-square test shows a significant statistical relationship between prison and proportion of participants for whom a problem of the type shown was identified as a key problem ($p < .05$).

A broad comparison between Tables 6.1 and 6.2 and the OASys results shown in Chapter 1, Table 1.2, indicates that the problems most often prioritised for intervention in the action plans – drugs, accommodation and thinking skills – were among those most often identified as significant in OASys assessments. Moreover, the differences between sites in targeted problems broadly reflected differences in their OASys results. This suggests reassuringly that action planning was generally related to assessed need. However, there were also some striking differences, most notably in that the area of 'lifestyle and associates' was assessed as a 'significant' problem in 75% of OASys assessments carried out, but was highlighted as a focus for intervention in only about a third of action plans (and as a top priority in only 5%). Similarly, 'attitudes' came out as the third most commonly assessed problem (52% of cases), but was well down the list in terms of action plans. This may be because both of the above tend to be considered as somewhat imprecisely defined and general problems, as opposed to something more 'concrete' such as drug addiction or lack of accommodation, for which it is easier to identify specific kinds of remedial intervention.

As noted earlier, a further feature of the action plans is some evident differences between the three sites in their prioritisation of problems to be addressed. For example, as Table 6.2 shows, drugs was by far the most common 'number one priority' in Hull (40% of prisoners), whereas accommodation issues were much more prominent in Lewes (38%) than elsewhere. Again, Parc prioritised 'thinking skills' (27%) more frequently than the other two sites, especially Lewes (4%). To

Table 6.2: Problems identified as the highest priority, by site (%) [a]

Problem	Parc	Lewes	Hull	All sites
Drugs	29	30	40	33
Accommodation[b]	14	38	7	18
Thinking skills[b]	27	4	18	17
Alcohol[b]	12	18	5	11
Lifestyle and associates	3	–	10	5
Education/training	2	5	5	4
Attitudes	6	1	5	4
Employment	1	3	6	3
Emotional well-being	4	–	1	2
Financial management	2	–	2	1
Relationships	1	1	2	1
Total	101	100	101	99

Notes:
$n = 281$. Percentages do not always total 100 due to rounding.
[a] Highest priority is defined as those problems listed as 'key problem one' on the CMR.
[b] Chi-square test shows a significant statistical relationship between prison and proportion of participants for whom a problem of the type shown was identified as the highest priority ($p < .05$). It should be noted that from 'lifestyle and associates' downwards, sample sizes were too small for the test to be reliable.

a large extent, such differences reflected the variations between sites in OASys scores discussed earlier, and underline once more (a) the differences in housing markets between the South East and other parts of the country and (b) the broad differences in emphasis between 'probation-led' and 'voluntary-led' programmes, which were also found in Phase 1 of the Resettlement Pathfinder evaluation (Lewis et al, 2003a, 2003b).

Case management

Examples of good case management practice were evident in all three sites. For example, both Hull and Lewes operated a simple but highly effective wall-mounted 'Cardex' system, which enabled the progress of any client to be tracked very quickly. In Parc, a tutor was assigned responsibility for all one-to-one contact and subsequent paperwork for half of the individuals in a programme, while his or her co-tutor took responsibility for case-managing the other half of the group. This increased consistency and helped to build a relationship between the tutors and the offenders for whom they were responsible.

Post-release continuity was helped in Hull by programme staff meeting participants in the community in addition to facilitating the programme in prison. Facilitators were thus responsible for case management 'through the gate'. As well as improving continuity of service, this greatly reduced gaps in the post-release record-keeping and CMRs were less likely to go missing.

Parc also held monthly meetings, to which all FOR probation links were invited, in order to improve the case management process during the post-release phase of the programme. These meetings were primarily held to discuss any post-release contact made and issues affecting the smooth running of the programme, both pre- and post-release. Further, copies of work undertaken in session 13 were forwarded to community links, thus increasing their knowledge of each individual who made contact. While the community tutors at Lewes felt that they had received some support and feedback from the prison, it was generally felt that post-release progress would have been greatly improved if they had organised monthly team meetings for all FOR staff.

Pre-release attrition

As noted earlier, 21% of all participants who started the FOR programme failed to complete it. This is a higher drop-out rate than is usually found in offending behaviour programmes for longer-term prisoners, such as Enhanced Thinking Skills, which often experience rates under 10%. Four factors were identified as contributing to attrition from FOR, although the last two were relatively infrequent:

- Home Detention Curfew (HDC);
- delays in the programme;
- segregation;
- voluntary drop-out.

The case management records showed that early release under the HDC system was the primary reason for failures to complete the programme. Attrition for this reason was also said by project staff to have increased after the maximum period of HDC (on condition of electronic tagging) was extended from 60 to 90 days:

> 'You've got HDC which is now being extended and it's probably going to be extended again, they're the same people that we're trying to get prior to release on this programme, so you find it difficult to actually get this group up and running.'

In an attempt to ameliorate this problem, the project team in Parc developed an 'early warning system' to identify as quickly as possible those about to be granted HDC,[2] and to have contingency arrangements in place to maximise the chances of FOR staff maintaining post-release contact with those released early.

---

[2] One of the FOR tutors was also the HDC clerk, and routinely let the FOR team know about likely releases.

Programme delays were also responsible for a number of failed completions. In particular, during the early stages of the evaluation, the FOR programme in Lewes did not always run to schedule, due primarily to temporary staffing problems. As a result, a small number of participants were released before all 12 sessions could be delivered. When this happened, the team at Lewes provided the offender with telephone numbers and addresses of community agencies prior to release, and encouraged him to remain in contact for further support.

Only small numbers of participants were sent to the segregation unit, but when this happened, programme staff had very little control over whether they could return to attend sessions.

In short, most of the attrition that occurred was unavoidable. The number of participants that voluntarily dropped out of the programme was extremely low. Indeed, it was known for participants to cancel or rearrange visits and appointments in order to attend programme sessions.

Arrangements for post-release contact

It was clear from interviews with project staff in all three sites that relationships with outside service providers had become stronger over the period of the Pathfinders, and that the session 12 'Marketplace' provided an excellent opportunity for prisoners to make firm appointments for post-release assistance directly with the relevant local agencies. The Hull team was the most enthusiastic of the three about the way in which this system worked in practice. One of the managers stated:

> 'I feel quite proud of the fact that every time we have a Marketplace, they are people that I have personally made links with and we have a really good relationship with outside agencies, absolutely wonderful, 100%.'

In both Parc and Lewes, one of the tutors was assigned the specific responsibility for maintaining working relations and coordinating links with the agencies. Their principal duty within this role was to set up the Marketplace session with the agencies and organise access for their workers to come into the prison to attend session 12.

Nevertheless, by no means all the arrangements operated as smoothly as had been planned. Notwithstanding the best efforts of the Lewes team, poor agency commitment was often evident, particularly with regard to agencies operating outside the Brighton area (and within the two remaining catchment areas, Worthing and Eastbourne). Moreover, post-release tutors often failed to attend the Marketplace. These problems were partly addressed by the Brighton agencies providing referrals and advice across all three areas. However, it was felt that by replicating the example set by the FOR team in Hull and establishing a formal partnership with a mentoring agency in the local area, relationships with local service providers and the monitoring of service uptake would be improved.

Similarly, the need to draw up a contract or formal agreement aimed at consolidating agency commitment to the programme was also commented upon by staff at Parc. This would effectively make agencies more accountable to the programme and increase the likelihood that representatives attended session 12 and honoured appointments made with prisoners.

As shown in Chapters 4 and 5, levels of post-release contact among short sentence (Automatic Unconditional Release, AUR) prisoners were found to be fairly high in Hull, but – despite the efforts of community links to establish contact with prisoners prior to their release – disappointingly low in the other two sites. Various attempts were made by both these projects to improve the situation, including sending letters and telephoning prisoners to remind them what support was available and how to contact their community link. Such methods bore some fruit: several offenders attended appointments as a result, while tutors also received letters and telephone calls from ex-FOR participants informing them of their progress in the community and thanking them for their help. Nevertheless, the difference in contact levels between these two prisons and Hull remained striking.

The explanation for this difference may be partly to do with the geographical locations of the probation offices. In Hull, virtually all of the participants lived relatively near to the office and thus may have been more inclined to make contact due to the ease of access. By contrast, the large geographical catchment area covered by the teams in Parc and Lewes may have contributed to the low levels of voluntary contact achieved, as offenders in these sites may not have had the means (or sufficient commitment) to travel to one of the probation offices linked with the FOR programme.

However, the higher rates of voluntary contact achieved in Hull may also be explained, in large part, by the post-release model that operated at this site. As outlined earlier, the FOR tutors (supervised by a throughcare manager) were also responsible for meeting ex-prisoners in the community. Weekly drop-in sessions were run where they could receive help with practical problems (such as housing and benefits) and/or emotional support. Staff felt that by assuming the role of community contact in addition to facilitating the programme, they provided vital continuity for participants, many of whom saw the post-release contact as a continuation of the programme:

> 'We maintain a relationship from the first moment we see these people on the first contact and maintain that right the way through to the post-release. We have realised that they are more happy coming to see people whom they have dealt with in prison.'

Even when regular contact was maintained, however, staff in all three sites expressed frustration at the problems encountered by prisoners when attempting to access services post-release. A general lack of service provision and long waiting lists were widely cited as factors likely to impact negatively upon prisoners' motivation. Such difficulties were especially salient for drug and alcohol services, many of which had waiting lists in excess of six months:

> 'There are awful long waiting lists especially for those with alcohol issues, it is very demotivating for those who have asked to do some kind of rehab work only to be told there is a 12-month waiting list. There aren't enough services out there, we do the best with what we have got.'

In addition, the staff at Lewes drew attention to the extreme shortage of adequate housing in the East Sussex area:

> 'There is no housing in the area. The housing they set up is places like [a named run-down hotel] which are full of people that are newly off the street, using drugs etc, etc, it's totally emergency housing and we have no means of getting people into what I would call some kind of safe housing such as their own flats or bedsits in reasonable areas.'

Finally, staff in all three sites were familiar (from the previous Pathfinders) with the difficulties associated with monitoring service uptake, and various attempts were made to improve the quality of information about post-release agency contact. A structured approach was adopted at Parc, whereby agencies were asked to complete contact sheets listing the names of prisoners they had seen at the Marketplace session: this made it easier to follow up cases post-release to see if offers of services had actually been taken up. A reasonably efficient tracking system was also in place at Hull, whereby the Pathfinder PSO was responsible for following up community contacts. Additionally, the close working relationship between the FOR team and their mentor scheme (Humbercare) assisted the team in monitoring post-release agency contact. Quarterly reports were also submitted in all three sites, indicating which participants had kept appointments, and the outcomes of these appointments.

Conclusions

his final chapter draws together the main findings from the research, focusing particularly on those which relate to issues of effectiveness, both in the delivery of services and (as far as can be determined) outcomes, and highlighting possible implications for the future development of resettlement services.

The FOR programme: quality and delivery

A detailed study of the quality and integrity of the delivery of the FOR programme yielded encouraging results for all three sites. Levels of integrity were high and the tutors delivered the programme well. The programme was assessed by the researchers who observed it in action as coherent and systematically focused on motivation, with a robust design capable of accommodating different styles of facilitation. The necessary element of directiveness to maintain the engagement of the participants is supported by the structure and sequence of the programme. Some practical difficulties arose with session 13, which is meant to be delivered as a group session but close to release: this, however, was often impractical as group members had different release dates. Some facilitators changed it to an individual session.

The programme appeared to be successful in stimulating individual prisoners to work on specific personal goals and to identify potential obstacles, and it was for the most part enthusiastically received and well understood by participants. Interviews with staff and prisoners about the programme found broadly positive attitudes in both groups, and prisoners' comments about what they learned from the programme were mostly in line with its aims. These findings tend to support its wider use in supporting resettlement work.

Implementation issues

In all three sites, staff were able to offer the FOR programme to substantial numbers of prisoners, coming close to their original target of 300 completions during the second phase. Altogether, 352 prisoners started the programme and 278 (79%) completed it during the study period. The main reason for non-completion was early release on Home Detention Curfew.

We were not able to collect accurate data on the number of eligible prisoners in each site (that is, prisoners in the appropriate sentence categories who were being released to the local area) but it is likely that the projects varied in the proportions of potential participants they were able to involve: in the previous Pathfinders, the proportions of short-term prisoners joining the projects among those known to be eligible varied between 97% and 65%, while in prisons running FOR it was estimated that about 10% of all those eligible completed the programme (Lewis et al, 2003a). It is likely that this latter figure was surpassed – and perhaps doubled where short-termers are concerned – in Phase 2.

One finding which raised concern – and which reflected the situation found in the earlier Pathfinders – was an under-representation among FOR participants of black and minority ethnic prisoners. This problem – which has also been noted in relation to offending behaviour programmes more generally (NACRO, 2002; Powis and Walmsley, 2002; Calverley et al, 2004) – clearly needs to be addressed if the programme is to make its full contribution to addressing resettlement problems. In addition to obvious issues of equity, it is important because black and minority ethnic prisoners have consistently been found to have more acute resettlement problems than white prisoners (see, for example, Maguire et al, 1997; NACRO, 2000, 2002). Possible remedies include systematic monitoring of recruitment and referral, regular reviews of programme content and the involvement where possible of minority ethnic staff in delivery.

A survey of agencies likely to receive referrals from the projects – most of which were regular attenders at the Marketplace session – revealed a generally positive attitude to the programme. On the other hand, some project staff commented that prisoners' motivation could be undermined on release by poor services to follow this up.

Impact and outcomes

The average level of 'continuity of service' (defined as contact with the project beyond the day of release) achieved among short-term prisoners in the present study exceeded the figures available for post-release contact in voluntary aftercare in the 1990s (Maguire et al, 1997) but did not exceed those reported in the 'seven-Pathfinder' study (Lewis et al, 2003a, 2003b). Marked variations in post-release contact rates across the three sites appeared to be related to different ways of managing post-release contact, rather than differences in the prisoner populations or in levels of quality of programme delivery. The highest continuity was achieved in Hull, where 29% of FOR 'starters' and 41% of 'completers' made some face-to-face contact with project staff after release. This may be partly a consequence of the smaller geographical area within which Hull prisoners tended to resettle, and partly of Hull's model of using prison-based programme facilitators to see offenders (many of whom they have got to know well in custody) after release. By contrast, the lowest rates were found in Parc, where contact responsibility was passed to an outside probation officer. In Lewes the contact role was shared by facilitators and community workers based outside the prison: here, levels of continuity were higher than Parc but lower than Hull. These findings emphasise the importance of a well-organised post-release service with as much continuity of personal contact as possible.

Among Automatic Conditional Release (ACR) prisoners, for whom post-release contact was obligatory, no significant differences were found in compliance rates (avoidance of breach of licence) between those who participated in the programme and locally generated comparison groups who had not.

All three sites showed significant positive changes in attitudes and self-reported problems (as measured by the CRIME-PICS II 'G' and 'P' scales), and the changes between entering the projects and the point of release were larger than those reported in the previous seven-Pathfinder study. Unlike that study, the present evaluation also included useful numbers of third assessments of attitudes and problems made some time after release. These showed maintenance of initial gains, with some further improvements (although, of course, less successful ex-prisoners may have been less likely to be available for assessment). These findings are consistent with the hypothesis that the programme has positive effects on attitudes and on approaches to problems, and support the general finding of the first study that effective resettlement services must address thinking and motivation as well as practical needs (Lewis et al, 2003a; see also Zamble and Quinsey, 1997). However, the absence of a control group for the CRIME-PICS scores, and possible selection effects, mean that these results cannot be treated as conclusive.

It should also be noted that young offenders in the study showed less change; this finding, again, should be viewed with caution, as their numbers were small, but it may deserve further investigation.

Some information was gathered from post-release case management records (CMRs) on, and interviews with, FOR participants to shed more light on some other desired outcomes of the programme, including improvements in accommodation, employment and substance misuse, and reductions in self-reported re-offending. None of the findings can be taken as conclusive: those on whom information was available did not constitute a random sample of those in the projects, since the more settled and successful individuals are more likely to keep in touch with staff and to be contactable for interviews. It is also possible that some of those interviewed presented an exaggeratedly rosy picture of their situation. Nevertheless, the CMR-based findings do indicate a substantial increase in levels of employment (pre-imprisonment to post-release) among the group of 97 on whom information was recorded, easily surpassing their own expectations. While the proportion in permanent accommodation fell, there were also indications of a decrease in the numbers homeless. Moreover, many of those interviewees who were successfully coping with resettlement problems stated that their experiences in the projects, and particularly the programme, had helped them to do this. It is also worth noting that, of 51 interviewees who reported that they had had a substance misuse problem before going to prison, 80% claimed that the programme had helped them to control it to some extent after release – principally by adopting a less harmful 'drug of choice'. Similarly, of the 70% of interviewees who claimed that they had not offended since release, 82% considered that the programme had helped them to achieve this.

Finally, the results of the one-year reconviction study of participants in the Phase 1 Pathfinders – which covered a variety of service models but included relatively small numbers of offenders who completed the FOR programme – offer some mixed messages. Again, these must be treated with caution owing to possible selection effects. When levels of risk were controlled for, the Pathfinders as a whole had no significant effect on one-year reconviction rates, either as predicted by OGRS2, or in relation to comparison groups drawn from the short-term populations of the same prisons a year earlier. At the same time, however, these broad-brush statements conceal several more positive results. Outcomes were highly variable across the Pathfinders, and both bi-variate and multi-variate analysis showed that certain groups among the participants were reconvicted at rates that were statistically significantly lower than predicted. Specifically:

- overall, participants who had post-release contact with any project staff or community links had significantly lower reconviction rates (relative to risk) than those who had no contact;
- as whole groups, prisoners who took part in the Springhill/Woodhill and Parc projects (both probation-led) did significantly better than those at other prisons;
- among prisoners who completed FOR, those who engaged in post-release work did significantly better than those who did not;
- prisoners from the Lewes and Wandsworth projects (both voluntary-led) who had post-release contact with mentors did significantly better than any other group of prisoners analysed;
- all the above-mentioned groups who 'did well' were also reconvicted at a lower rate (relative to risk) than prisoners in the comparison groups drawn from the relevant prison(s); however, only in the case of post-release contact with mentors did such differences reach the level of statistical significance.

Perhaps the clearest message to emerge from the reconviction findings is the importance of post-release contact to follow up work begun in custody. The positive results from Parc and Springhill/Woodhill (taken in conjunction with changes observed in attitudes to crime) also suggest that – while voluntary mentors may be more effective post-release – the involvement of probation officers inside prison may play an important part, by dint of their professional input and focus on motivation and thinking skills.

Although indicative rather than conclusive, these results suggest that two of the most promising components of a successful resettlement strategy, in terms of reducing reconviction, may be:

(a) work inside prison by professionally trained staff, particularly probation officers;
(b) post-release contact by people such as mentors (whose distinctive contribution is usually the offer of personal and emotional support).[1]

Whether or not the custodial phase of resettlement is likely to achieve lower reconviction rates by running a cognitive-motivational programme such as FOR is still an open question, but the results are promising at least in terms of attitude change.

---

[1] The establishment of such contact, it should be noted, appears to be more important than how long it lasts.

References

Banks, C. and Fairhead, S. (1976) *The Petty Short Term Prisoner,* London: Howard League For Penal Reform.

Bernfeld, G. (2001) 'The struggle for treatment integrity in a "dis-integrated" service delivery system', in G.A. Bernfeld, D.P. Farrington and A.W. Leschied (eds) *Offender Rehabilitation in Practice: Implementing and Evaluating Effective Programs,* Chichester: Wiley.

Bochel, D. (1976) *Probation and After-Care: Its Development in England and Wales,* Edinburgh: Scottish Academic Press.

Bonta, J., Bogue, B., Crowley, M. and Motiuk, L. (2001) 'Implementing offender classification systems: lessons learned', in G.A. Bernfeld, D.P. Farrington and A.W. Leschied (eds) *Offender Rehabilitation in Practice: Implementing and Evaluating Effective Programs,* Chichester: Wiley.

Caddle, D. and White, S. (1994) *The Welfare Needs of Unconvicted Prisoners,* Research and Planning Unit Paper No. 81, London: Home Office.

Calverley, A., Cole, B., Kaur, G., Lewis, S., Raynor, P., Sadeghi, S., Smith, D., Vanstone, M. and Wardak, A. (2004) *Black and Asian Offenders on Probation,* Home Office Research Study No. 277, London: Home Office.

Carlen, P. (1983) *Women's Imprisonment: A Study in Social Control,* London: Routledge and Kegan Paul.

Colledge, M., Collier, P. and Brand, S. (1999) *Programmes for Offenders: Guidance for Evaluators,* London: Home Office, Research Development and Statistics Department.

Copas, J., Ditchfield, J. and Marshall, P. (1994) 'Development of a new reconviction score', *Home Office Research Bulletin,* no 36, pp 30-7.

Corden, J. (1983) 'Persistent petty offenders: problems and patterns of multiple disadvantage', *Howard Journal of Criminal Justice,* vol XXII, pp 68-90.

Corden, J., Kuipers, J. and Wilson, K. (1978) *After Prison: A Study of Post-release experiences of Discharged Prisoners,* York: University of York, Department of Social Administration and Social Work.

Corden, J., Kuipers, J. and Wilson, K. (1979) 'Accommodation and homelessness on release from prison', *British Journal of Social Work,* vol 9, pp 75-86.

CSAP (Correctional Services Accreditation Panel) (2004) *The Correctional Services Accreditation Panel Report 2003-4,* London: Home Office, www.probation.homeoffice.gov.uk/files/pdf/CSAP_report03to04.pdf

Egan, G. (1990) *The Skilled Helper: A Systematic Approach to Effective Helping* (4th edn), Pacific Grove, CA: Brooks/Cole.

Fabiano, E. and Porporino, F. (2002) *Focus on Resettlement – A Change,* Canada: T3 Associates.

Fairhead, S. (1981) *Persistent Petty Offenders*, Home Office Research Study No. 66, London: HMSO.

Farrall, S. (2002) *Rethinking What Works with Offenders*, Cullompton, Devon: Willan.

Francis, B., Crosland, P. and Harman, J. (2002) *The Police National Computer and the Offenders Index: Can They be Combined for Research Purposes?, Findings 170*, London: Home Office.

Friendship, C., Thornton, D., Erikson, M. and Beech, A. (2001) 'Reconviction: a critique and comparison of two main data sources in England and Wales', *Legal and Criminal Psychology*, vol 6, no 1, pp 121-9.

Frude, N., Honess, T. and Maguire, M. (1994) *CRIME-PICS II Manual*, London: M&A.

Gendreau, P., Coggin, C. and Smith, P. (2001) 'Implementation guidelines for correctional programs in the "real world"', in G.A. Bernfeld, D.P. Farrington and A.W. Leschied (eds) *Offender Rehabilitation in Practice: Implementing and Evaluating Effective Programs*, Chichester: Wiley.

Ginsburg, J.I.D., Mann, R.E., Rotgers, F. and Weekes, J.R. (2002) 'Motivational interviewing with criminal justice populations', in W.R. Miller and S. Rollnick (eds) *Motivational Interviewing: Preparing People for Change* (2nd edn), New York, NY: Guilford Press.

Goldblatt, P. and Lewis, C. (1998) *Reducing Offending: An Assessment of Research Evidence on Ways of Dealing with Offending Behaviour*, Home Office Research Study No. 187, London: Home Office.

Halliday, J. (2001) *Making Punishments Work*, London: Home Office.

Hollin, C. (1995) 'The meaning and implications of "programme integrity"', in J. McGuire (ed) *What Works: Reducing Reoffending*, Chichester: Wiley.

Hollin, C. (2001) 'The role of the consultant in developing effective correctional programs', in G.A. Bernfeld, D.P. Farrington and A.W. Leschied (eds) *Offender Rehabilitation in Practice: Implementing and Evaluating Effective Programs*, Chichester: Wiley.

Home Office (1984) *Probation Service in England and Wales: Statement of National Objectives and Priorities*, London: Home Office.

Home Office (1992) *National Prison Survey 1991*, Home Office Research Study No. 128, London: HMSO.

Home Office (2001) *Through the Prison Gate: A Joint Thematic Review by HM Inspectorates of Prison and Probation*, London: Home Office.

Lewis, S., Vennard, J., Maguire, M., Raynor, P., Vanstone, M., Raybould, S. and Rix, A. (2003a) *The Resettlement of Short-term Prisoners: An Evaluation of Seven Pathfinders*, RDS Occasional Paper No. 83, London: Home Office.

Lewis, S., Maguire, M., Raynor, P., Vanstone, M. and Vennard, J. (2003b) *The Resettlement of Short-term Prisoners: An Evaluation of Seven Pathfinders, Findings 200*, London: Home Office.

Maguire, M. and Raynor, P. (1997) 'The revival of throughcare: rhetoric and reality in automatic conditional release', *British Journal of Criminology*, vol 37, pp 1-14.

Maguire, M. and Raynor, P. (2006) 'How the resettlement of prisoners promotes desistance from crime: or does it?', *Criminal Justice*, vol 6, no 1, pp 17-36.

Maguire, M., Raynor, P., Vanstone, M. and Kynch, J. (1997) *Voluntary Aftercare*, London: Home Office.

Maguire, M., Raynor, P., Vanstone, M. and Kynch, J. (2000) 'Voluntary aftercare and the probation service: a case of diminishing responsibility', *Howard Journal*, vol 39, pp 234-48.

Maruna, S. (2000) *Making Good*, Washington, DC: American Psychological Association.

McGuire, J. (1995) *What Works: Reducing Reoffending*, Chichester: Wiley.

Miller, W.R. and Rollnick, S. (1991) *Motivational Interviewing: Preparing People to Change Addictive Behaviours*, New York, NY: Guilford Press.

Miller, W.R. and Rollnick, S. (2002) *Motivational Interviewing: Preparing People for Change* (2nd edn), New York, NY: Guilford Press.

NACRO (National Association for the Care and Resettlement of Offenders) (1993) *Opening the Doors: The Resettlement of Prisoners in the Community*, London: NACRO.

NACRO (1996) *Women Prisoners: Towards a New Millennium*, London: NACRO.

NACRO (2000) *The Forgotten Majority: The Resettlement of Short-Term Prisoners*, London: NACRO.

NACRO (2002) *Resettling Prisoners from Black and Minority Ethnic Groups*, London: NACRO.

Nellis, M. (1995) 'Towards a new view of probation values', in R. Hugman and D. Smith (eds) *Ethical Issues in Social Work*, London: Routledge.

NPS (National Probation Service) (2001) *Offender Assessment System: User Manual*, London: NPS.

Page, L. (1950) *The Young Lag*, London: Faber and Faber.

Powis, B. and Walmsley, R. (2002) *Programmes for Black and Asian Offenders on Probation: Lessons for Developing Practice*, Research Study 250, London: Home Office.

Raynor, P. (1998) 'Attitudes, social problems and reconvictions in the STOP probation experiment', *Howard Journal*, vol 37, pp 1-15.

Raynor, P. and Maguire, M. (2006) 'End-to-end or end in tears? Prospects for the effectiveness of the National Offender Management Model', in M. Hough, R. Allen and U. Padel (eds) *Reshaping Probation and Prisons: The New Offender Management Framework*, Bristol: The Policy Press.

Raynor, P. and Vanstone, M. (1996) 'Reasoning and rehabilitation in Britain: the results of the Straight Thinking On Probation (STOP) programme', *International Journal of Offender Therapy and Comparative Criminology*, vol 40, pp 279-91.

Ross, R. and Fabiano, E. (1985) *Time to Think: A Cognitive Model of Delinquency Prevention and Offender Rehabilitation*, Johnson City, TN: Institute of Social Sciences and Arts.

Ross, R., Fabiano, E.A. and Ross, R.D. (1986) *Reasoning and Rehabilitation: A Handbook for Teaching Cognitive Skills*, Ottawa: AIR Training and Publications.

Rough Sleepers Unit (2000) *Blocking the Fast Track from Prison to Rough Sleeping*, London: Office of the Deputy Prime Minister (summarised online at www.odpm.gov.uk/index.asp?id=1150098).

Social Exclusion Unit (2002) *Reducing Re-offending by Ex-prisoners*, London: Office of the Deputy Prime Minister.

Vanstone, M. (2004) *Supervising Offenders in the Community: A History of Probation Theory and Practice*, Aldershot: Ashgate.

Zamble, E. and Quinsey, V. (1997) *The Criminal Recidivism Process*, Cambridge: Cambridge University Press.

Appendix

Supplementary tables and figures

Table A1: OASys scores, by site (prisoners starting FOR)

OASys score	<40 (%)	40-99 (%)	100+ (%)	Total (%)	Mean
Parc	13	60	27	100	77.7
Hull	5	45	50	100	96.0
Lewes	13	56	31	100	82.6
All sites	10	54	36	100	85.3

Notes:
n = 301.
Anova and Kruskal-Wallis tests show significant differences between sites (*p* < .01).

Table A2: Initial CRIME-PICS 'P' ('Problems') scores, by site (prisoners starting FOR)

CRIME-PICS P	<20 (%)	20-29 (%)	30-39 (%)	40+ (%)	Total (%)	Mean
Parc	11	40	27	22	100	31.2
Hull	12	38	30	20	100	30.5
Lewes	4	25	36	35	100	36.1
All sites	10	36	30	24	100	32.2

Notes:
n = 303.
Anova and Kruskal-Wallis tests show significant differences between sites (*p* < .01).

Table A3: Initial CRIME-PICS 'G' ('Attitudes') scores, by site (prisoners starting FOR)

CRIME-PICS G	<30 (%)	30-39 (%)	40-49 (%)	50+ (%)	Total (%)	Mean
Parc	15	20	34	31	100	43.4
Hull	8	19	26	47	100	48.0
Lewes	4	21	27	48	100	48.4
All sites	10	20	29	41	100	46.4

Notes:
$n = 303$.
Anova and Kruskal-Wallis tests show significant differences between sites ($p < .01$)

Table A4: Self-reported employment status before sentence (and expected after release), by site (%)

	Employed prior to custody	Unemployed prior to custody	In training/ education/ inactive prior to custody	(Expecting to be employed on release)	Total
Parc	29	62	9	(29)	100
Hull	15	83	3	(7)	101
Lewes	27	64	9	(22)	100
All sites	23	70	7	(19)	100

Notes:
$n = 281$.
Percentages do not always total 100 due to rounding.
Relevant information was recorded on only 281 of the 352 prisoners who started FOR, but there were no obvious differences in characteristics between those on whom data were and were not recorded.

Table A5: Self-reported accommodation status before sentence (and expected after release), by site (%)

	Permanent prior to custody	Transient prior to custody	No fixed abode prior to custody	Other prior to custody	(Expecting to go to permanent on release)	Total
Parc	42	24	9	26	(34)	101
Hull	49	33	18	0	(41)	100
Lewes	36	33	23	8	(29)	100
All sites	43	30	16	11	(35)	100

Notes:
n = 281.
Percentages do not always total 100 due to rounding.
Relevant information was recorded on only 281 of the 352 prisoners who started FOR, but there were no obvious differences in characteristics between those on whom data were and were not recorded.

Table A6: Phase 2 Pathfinders: regression model predicting high continuity of service

Variable	Exp (B)	Sig.
Hull	3.75	*
Parc	–	–
Lewes	–	–
Aged < 30	–	–
OASys score > 100	–	–

Notes:
n = 125 offenders who completed the FOR programme in custody.
* denotes significance at the 5% level.

Table A7: Predicted and actual one-year reconviction rates of male participants who had post-release contact with a mentor or other FOR staff, or no contact (%)

	Intervention groups			Comparison groups		
	One-year reconviction rate			One-year reconviction rate		
Post-release contact[a]	Predicted	Actual	Actual minus predicted			
Contact with mentor	55	42	−13			
Contact with other	48	49	+1			
No contact	53	59	+6			
				Predicted	Actual	Actual minus predicted
All male participants	52	55	+3	43	45	+2
Wandsworth and Lewes[b]				43	45	+2

Notes:

Intervention groups: contact with mentor n = 55, with other n = 236, no contact n = 473, all males n = 764, Wandsworth and Lewes n = 261.

Comparison groups: all males n = 1,542, Wandsworth and Lewes n = 591.

[a] In the intervention groups, differences between (actual minus predicted) reconviction rates in the three categories of post-release contact were statistically significant (Kruskal-Wallis test p = . 006).

[b] The difference between the (actual minus predicted) reconviction rate for post-release contact with a mentor, and that for the comparison group from Lewes/Wandsworth, was statistically significant (t-test p = .015).

Figure A1: Phase 1 Pathfinders: differences between actual and predicted one-year reconviction rates: participants with and without post-release contact, by prison

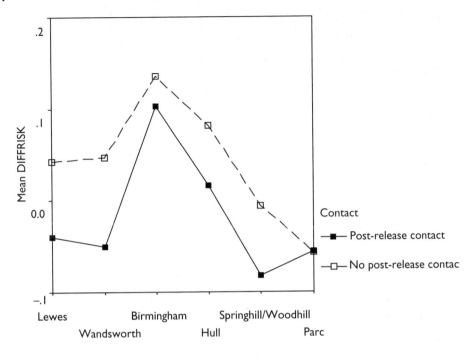

Note:
DIFFRISK = Actual minus predicted one-year reconviction rate. A score below 0 signifies a lower reconviction rate than predicted.

Appendix

Headings of the 13 sessions in the 'FOR – A Change' programme

Session 1: From the Inside Out
Session 2: Looking Forward
Session 3: Current State: A New Perspective
Session 4: Six Thinking Shades
Session 5: Understanding Needs and Wants
Session 6: Setting Goals
Session 7: Establishing SMART Goals
Session 8: Moving Forward, Developing a Personal Change Plan
Session 9: Tipping the Balance
Session 10: My Personal Change Plan
Session 11: Steps Toward Action
Session 12: Accessing the Community Resources Marketplace [within two weeks of release, with invited agency representatives and community links]
Session 13: Free to Change [pre-release individual session]

Appendix

Conversion of OGRS2 24-month predicted reconviction rates into 12-month predictions

There is no established way of converting the 24-month reconviction rates predicted by 'Offender Group Reconviction Scale' (OGRS2) scores into 12-month reconviction predictions, which do not stand in a simple relationship to each other. However, Copas et al (1994) provide a table of observed 12-month reconviction rates for prediction scores from the first version of OGRS, from which we have created a 'conversion table' for OGRS2 scores. A similar exercise was undertaken in the Straight Thinking on Probation (STOP) programme evaluation by Raynor and Vanstone (1996).

The Copas et al table provides observed rates for 32 percentage values, leaving a need to estimate rates for the remainder. An initial regression of these 32 values suggested that the quadratic fit was good (adjusted $R^2 > .99$), but examination of the plot showed that the observed values tended to be slightly above the curve for lower values, and below it at higher values, with a 'threshold' at 60. It was also poor at the extremes (close to 0 or 100). We improved on the overall fit by splitting the values, giving the following equations for a model estimator:

Recon12 = 0.089823 + (0.503852) recon24 + (0.003207) recon24**2, where recon12 = 12-month observed value; recon24 = 24-month OGRS value; and recon24 < 60

Recon12 = 93.872402 − (2.217422) recon24 + (0.022844) recon24**2, where recon24 $\geq$ 60

These equations were used to create a conversion table for all possible values, as reproduced below. The model estimates were adjusted to smooth transitional values between the observed 12-month rates. The maximum difference of the model estimates from the observed values was ±1%. Our final adjusted estimates were used in the analysis in the report.

Table C1: OGRS 24-month and estimated 12-month reconviction rates (%)

OGRS 24-month reconviction	Estimated 12-month reconviction		OGRS 24-month reconviction	Estimated 12-month reconviction
1	1		51	34
2	1		52	35
3	2		53	36
4	2		54	37
5	3		55	37
6	3		56	39
7	4		57	39
8	4		58	40
9	5		59	41
10	5		60	42
11	6		61	43
12	7		62	44
13	7		63	44
14	8		64	45
15	8		65	47
16	9		66	47
17	10		67	48
18	10		68	49
19	11		69	50
20	11		70	51
21	12		71	52
22	13		72	53
23	13		73	55
24	14		74	56
25	15		75	57
26	15		76	58
27	16		77	60
28	17		78	61
29	17		79	62
30	18		80	63
31	19		81	64
32	19		82	66
33	20		83	67

OGRS 24-month reconviction	Estimated 12-month reconviction	OGRS 24-month reconviction	Estimated 12-month reconviction
34	21	84	68
35	22	85	69
36	22	86	71
37	23	87	73
38	24	88	75
39	25	89	76
40	25	90	78
41	26	91	80
42	27	92	83
43	28	93	85
44	28	94	87
45	29	95	89
46	30	96	92
47	31	97	95
48	32	98	96
49	32	99	98
50	33	100	100

Appendix

Prediction of reconvictions: OGRS2, OASys and CRIME-PICS II

In this Appendix, we consider the performance of OGRS2, OASys and CRIME-PICS II in the prediction of reconviction over a 12-month period.

OGRS2 is well established as a predictor of reconviction over two years from static factors: in this study, OGRS2 scores were converted into one-year predictions (see Appendix C). This provided a 'benchmark' with which to compare OASys and CRIME-PICS II. It was decided to test each of the instruments on the same group of offenders. All the relevant scores were available for a total of 475 male and 79 female offenders. However, the female group was too small for reliable analysis.

As shown in Table D1, for males, the 12-month OGRS had a fairly high correlation with the OASys total scores, and with the 'G' (attitudes to offending) scores from CRIME-PICS II, but much lower correlation with the 'P' (perception of problems) scale.

Table D1: Correlation of OASys and CRIME-PICS II 'G' scores with 12-month prediction score derived from OGRS2 (n = 475 males)

	Pearson R^2	Significance of correlation
OASys score	.635	.000
CRIME-PICS 'G' score	.467	.000
CRIME-PICS 'P' score	.245	.000

Each of the three main predictors (12-month OGRS, OASys and CRIME-PICS II 'G') was then assessed for successful prediction of one-year reconviction, using logistic regression. Table D2 shows the performance of each in terms of the percentage of male offenders who were correctly predicted to reconvict or not to reconvict.

Table D2: Correct prediction of reconviction or no reconviction over 12-month period (n = 475 males)

	Correctly predicted % total			Nagelkerke R^2
	To reconvict	Not to reconvict	Overall	
12-month OGRS2 score	79	67	73	0.34
OASys score	76	61	69	0.24
CRIME-PICS 'G' score	71	61	66	0.18

All scores performed significantly better than chance, although the 'explanatory value' as measured by the Nagelkerke R^2 was not very great for either of the dynamic instruments.

Also available from The Policy Press

Youth crime and youth justice
Public opinion in England and Wales
Mike Hough and Julian V. Roberts

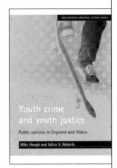

This report presents the findings from the first national, representative survey of public attitudes to youth crime and youth justice in England and Wales. It carries clear policy implications in relation to both public education and reform of the youth justice system.

Paperback £14.99 ISBN 1 86134 649 2
245 x 170mm 80 pages November 2004

From dependency to work
Addressing the multiple needs of offenders with drug problems
Tim McSweeney, Victoria Herrington, Mike Hough, Paul J. Turnbull and Jim Parsons

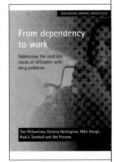

This report presents the findings from one of the first evaluations of a British programme to integrate drug and alcohol treatment with mental health services, and education, training and employment support – the 'From Dependency to Work (D2W)' programme. It provides an invaluable insight into the challenges and difficulties of integrating services in this way and highlights important lessons for central and regional government on funding and working with the voluntary sector to deliver services.

Paperback £14.99 ISBN 1 86134 660 3
245 x 170mm 88 pages December 2004

Plural policing
The mixed economy of visible patrols in England and Wales
Adam Crawford, Stuart Lister, Sarah Blackburn and Jonathan Burnett

This timely and important report draws together the findings of an extensive two-year study of developments in the provision of visible policing in England and Wales. Exploring the dynamic relations between different public and private providers, it combines an overview of national developments with a detailed analysis of six focused case studies, including two city centres, one out-of-town shopping centre, an industrial park and two residential areas.

Paperback £14.99 ISBN 1 86134 671 9
245 x 170mm 128 pages March 2005

Integrating victims in restorative youth justice
Adam Crawford and Tom Burden

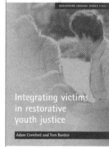

It is a key aim of current youth justice policy to introduce principles of restorative justice and involve victims in responses to crime. This is most evident in the referral order and youth offender panels established by the Youth Justice and Criminal Evidence Act 1999. However, the challenges involved in delivering a form of restorative youth justice that is sensitive to the needs of victims are considerable. This report provides an illuminating evaluation of the manner in which one Youth Offending Service sought to integrate victims into the referral order process.

Paperback £14.99 ISBN 1 86134 785 5
245 x 170mm 120 pages November 2005

Reshaping probation and prisons
The new offender management framework
Mike Hough, Rob Allen and Una Padel

The Government has embarked on a programme of radical reform for the probation and prison services with the setting up of a National Offender Management Service (NOMS). This groundbreaking volume takes a critical look at the different aspects of the NOMS proposals, at a time when the Government is still working out the detail of its reforms.

Paperback £14.99 ISBN 1 86134 812 6
245 x 170mm 112 pages January 2006

To order further copies of this publication or any other Policy Press titles please visit **www.policypress.org.uk** or contact:

In the UK and Europe:
Marston Book Services, PO Box 269, Abingdon, Oxon,
OX14 4YN, UK
Tel: +44 (0)1235 465500
Fax: +44 (0)1235 465556
Email: direct.orders@marston.co.uk

In the USA and Canada:
ISBS, 920 NE 58th Street, Suite 300, Portland,
OR 97213-3786, USA
Tel: +1 800 944 6190 (toll free)
Fax: +1 503 280 8832
Email: info@isbs.com

In Australia and New Zealand:
DA Information Services, 648 Whitehorse Road
Mitcham,
Victoria 3132, Australia
Tel: +61 (3) 9210 7777
Fax: +61 (3) 9210 7788
E-mail: service@dadirect.com.au

Further information about all of our titles can be found on our website.